TESTI.

"It is not often in life that we encounter someone who is so positive and so passionate that you truly can't wait until the next time you see them in person, hear them speak or read something that they have written. Dave Luehr is indeed one of these individuals. Filled with insight on the past, the present and the future, Dave Luehr is definitely someone who contributes to all that is good in the collision repair industry."

Mike Anderson, *Collision Advice*

"Stacey and Dave have done an extraordinary job analyzing, communicating insights and showcasing the best practices of the collision repair industry. This book is a must read for anyone who wants to understand the evolution of one of the most important industries in the American business world. Anyone from insurers to OEMs and from consumers to repair shops will benefit from this masterpiece."

Jose R. Costa, *Group President, Driven Brands*

"Dave Luehr has knocked it out of the park with this book. In my forty years as a shop owner, teacher and coach I rarely have read such a thoughtful and relevant masterpiece. Dave helps us see the current state of the collision repair industry in a kind and yet eye-opening way. Additionally, he offers hope for those of us who love our industry and coaches us into seeing even greater opportunity. Thank you Dave, I will recommend it to all of our students and coaching associates."

Dave Dunn, *CCRM, Founder of Masters School of Autobody Management and Dave's Auto Body*

THE SECRETS OF AMERICA'S GREATEST BODY SHOPS

THE SECRETS OF AMERICA'S GREATEST BODY SHOPS

*The book that will challenge everything you
know about the collision repair business*

DAVE LUEHR AND STACEY PHILLIPS

The Secrets of America's Greatest Body Shops

FIRST EDITION

ISBN-13: 9780692851784
ISBN-10 : 069285178X
Cover photo: Rydell Collision Center's Randy Sattler (left) in the body shop with Tom Tracy, Tracy's Collision Centers

To Dr. Susan Murray
A teacher who believed in me

TABLE OF CONTENTS

ACKNOWLEDGEMENTS

This book, most definitely, would not have been possible without the selfless contributions of many people. Some of these contributions came in the form of the direct creation of the book, while many others through inspiration, mentorship, and not to mention, the knowledge I've obtained over my many years in the collision repair industry. I am extremely grateful and humbled by those who have helped make this book possible and given me the encouragement to turn my dreams and this book into reality.

First, I want to thank the shop owners who found the time and courage to share their stories with the world. These individuals truly do run some of America's greatest body shops and all of them exemplify the positive mindset and attributes necessary to run a highly-successful collision repair business in our modern times. Much thanks to Dan Stander, Bruce King, Chris King, Randy Sattler, Tom Tracy, Tony Adams and Camille Eber.

I was deeply humbled by the positive responses by many indus-try experts offering to help however they could to make this book come to life. Highly respected individuals such as Brad Mewes, Steve Trapp, Jeff Peevy, Petra Schroder, Elainna Sachire, Brandon Eckenrode, and Aaron Schulenburg spent consider-able time contributing valuable content to this project. Special thanks also to Steve Schoolcraft and his team who spent many hours teaching us how to attract and keep customers for life.

A big thank you to my franchise friends who contribute great value to our industry and this book: Jonathan Herrera at Fix Auto, Melissa Miller at CARSTAR, and Jim Keller at 1Collision.

There were several suppliers who we featured in the book that we feel are very relevant to a shop's success now and in the future. Several of these companies are preferred suppliers of products or services to many of America's greatest body shops. Thanks to Jon Parker and Neil Parr-Davies from Body Shop Revolution, along with Patrick O'Neill at Bodyshop Express. Thanks also to Ryan Taylor of Bodyshop Booster and Jake Rodenroth of Collision Diagnostic Service (as-Tech), as well as to the owner of Lean Tec, Brandon Clift.

The collision repair business has been my life for over thirty years now, and it would never have started without my dear friends, Clark and Paula Luse, who gave me my first real job—thank you!

As a young entrepreneur, I was very fortunate to have several mentors who took me under their wing and taught me the ropes. Thanks Ken and Rhona Lovegrove, as well as Janet Chaney for being great influences in my life. I also want to acknowledge the man who helped me go from technician to businessman, and inspired me to eventually become a business coach and consultant from a very young age. Dave Williams, I will forever be in your debt.

To this day, I feel I have a tremendous support system within the industry and several people who have both inspired me and continue to help guide my career. Ron Kuehn, your friendship and mentorship have been amazing and I owe a great deal of my operational knowledge to your teaching. I also want to thank Mike Monaghan for showing me a better way to help collision repairers by "fixing" their mindset first. Mike Anderson, thanks for showing me the path; your contributions to this industry are immeasurable. Special thanks also to Kevin Wolfe, my success coach, who reminds me frequently how vast and beautiful human potential can be.

I also want to thank my family for their support. The process of writing a book often involves evenings and weekends, and I appreciate and love you for your understanding and support.

There have been many new friends and supporters since this project started, and I want to make sure they know how much I appreciate everything they have done for us during this project. Thanks to Shawn McLaughlin at McLaughlin Creative for all his hard work; he is a master when it comes to branding and was very helpful with our website. The fine folks at *Autobody News* have been a huge help with promoting the book and offering advice and encouragement. Also, Linda at eFrog Press was a tremendous asset as we navigated through the unchartered territories of being first-time authors. Thanks also to Victoria Antonelli who skillfully copy edited this project through late nights under a very short deadline.

Thanks to David Praet, who after an I-CAR meeting in Nashville, Tennessee, said, "Dave, you know what you need to do?" I told him I did not, to which he said, "You need to write a book!" This got my mind thinking about it. It was when I met my co-writer, Stacey Phillips, at the 2016 NACE event in Anaheim, California, that gave me the final shove into what has been a tremendous journey together. She has been an amazing partner on this project by giving me the encouragement to continue, and providing highly-skilled editing and writing skills necessary to complete a project like this successfully. If my book reads well, I assure you it is because of her. Thank you so much Stacey!

   – Dave Luehr

• • •

I want to thank Jeremy Hayhurst, Barbara Davies and the entire staff at *Autobody News* magazine for educating me about the collision repair industry and introducing me to so many wonderful people.

A big thank you to my two sons, Joseph and Jack, for being so supportive throughout the entire project.

I greatly appreciate the enormous amount of time the body shop owners and industry experts spent talking to me and allowing me to share their stories for the book.

Most of all, I want to thank my partner, Dave Luehr, for asking me to join this journey with him. He has great wisdom and insight about the collision repair industry and I am honored to be part of this project. I hope that the messages we share are helpful to those in the industry and encourage shop owners and managers to continually improve their businesses and strengthen their teams so they can deliver an excellent product to customers.

– Stacey Phillips

FOREWORD

By Jeff Peevy, President, Automotive Management Institute

There have not been many books written about the collision repair industry and its complex challenges and tremendous opportunities. It was a bold step for Dave Luehr to take on this project, requiring countless hours of observation, study and courage. He has ultimately created a valuable collection of knowledge that is clear, to the point and if applied, can escalate a repair business to levels often considered unobtainable. Those who read it will benefit immensely and likely transform the way they see and run their businesses and personal lives.

Dave is more than qualified to write this book and share his work. He started, as many of us did, in entry-level positions, working his way through the industry, paying close attention along the way and learning from every experience. His qualifi-cations, however, go far beyond the typical industry experience and expertise, as he has studied the personal traits, attitudes and approaches of the most successful collision repair shop owners and managers.

I met Dave many years ago through a research project I was leading at the time on the impact technical training had on shop operational accuracies, efficiencies, and overall profitability. Being the curious observer that he is, he engaged me with numerous questions and then began to share his observations openly. Since that time, we have forged a friendship based on our passion and commitment to professional and personal excellence. Each time my team and I ran into an observation that on the surface didn't make sense, I consulted Dave and he always provided insight that proved to be part of the key to unlocking the question we had. Dave has continued to fascinate me with his unique and valuable perspectives and helped me by sharing his enormous wisdom. This book reflects much of that perspective and wisdom in an organized way.

Dave takes a comprehensive view of the industry from his years of studious observations, which will prove transformational to many who read it. This effort goes beyond the typical operational view and shares insights and observations on many things that are "hidden" within a repair business and its leadership that determine the outcome, good and bad. Many of us can relate to Dave's industry experiences, but few have captured the story told and important lessons learned as well as Dave has in this book.

Likewise, his company, Elite Body Shop Solutions LLC, is a by-product of these observations and lessons and has transformed many collision repair businesses from struggling efforts to profitable, sustainable enterprises.

The relevance of this book will become clear as you read the case studies that reinforce the principles Dave is outlining. The reader will quickly begin to appreciate the enormous amount of work "in the trenches" that influenced what is written here. Though many of the things discussed are a snapshot of our industry's current dynamics, readers will find it to be a valuable resource to be shared with future generations to inspire them to greatness as well. Thank you, Dave, for sharing this body of valuable work. Readers, enjoy, dream big, set unrealistic goals and apply this information.

INTRODUCTION

The call came at four o'clock Friday afternoon. The call that not only changed my life but also changed the lives of so many others in Middle Tennessee. I remember it well; it was a sunny and unusually pleasant day for a February in Tennessee. Our location manager at Bradshaw Collision Centers, Brandy, approached me and several others as I was performing a training session out in the back parking lot at our Franklin store. She said that we would all need to meet in the break room at promptly four o'clock because our owner, Mr. Bradshaw, wanted to hold a conference call with the entire team. I asked her what the call was about, but she didn't say. The joy of our crisp sunny day suddenly took on a more ominous gloom. As a "trusted" member of the company's upper management team, I immediately wondered why Mr. Bradshaw had not reached out to me directly about this and instead confided in a location manager to break the news. My mind quickly jumped to conclude that "Oh my God we've been bought out!" Rumors had circulated around Nashville for several years about one of the big collision repair companies coming to town, but I would have to wait two more hours to find out for sure.

Promptly at four, bodymen, painters, estimators, and Brandy and I all shuffled into the tiny and cramped employee break room. The phone was placed on speaker so everyone could hear. It was exactly as I feared. It was the voice of Duane Rouse, the CEO of ABRA Auto Body & Glass, a large company based out of Minnesota. In the professional and inviting tone you would expect from a polished CEO, he broke the news not only to those of us crammed in the tiny break room but to the other eighty employees at four other locations also on the call. We had been bought out and by Monday morning we would cease to be Bradshaw's, and if what Mr. Rouse said was true, we would all be invited to join the ABRA team.

The stunned faces in the room mirrored my own. Others began to look to me for answers. "How long have you known this was going to happen?" I was asked by someone. I am not sure what I was angrier about, the company being sold, or just the fact that Mr. Bradshaw didn't tell me this would occur. I was embarrassed that I didn't know any more than the guys in the break room with me and unable to answer their questions. It was an ego thing I guess. I had studied ABRA's business model for many years and was familiar with their operations. All I could offer the team at the Franklin location was the encouragement that ABRA was a good company and everybody would be fine, even though deep down inside, I was full of doubt and fear for my job security. Upper management often is shown the door in these circumstances.

The transformation was not easy—especially for me. Bradshaw's had been in business since 1967, and as ABRA would quickly find out, was pretty set in its old Southern ways. I knew well of this resistance from my efforts during the previous two years while taking the entire organization through an extensive operational overhaul. Little did I know that my efforts were more about helping the company drive up its sales price than anything long term I had hoped for.

ABRA preferred the "rip off the Band-Aid" approach to integration for its largest single acquisition up to this point in history. ABRA sent in an army of people from all over the country and by Monday morning, we were no longer Bradshaw's. All five locations had new computer systems in place. Trainers were standing by to teach everyone the new ABRA way. I watched with admitted disdain, as members of the ABRA transition team were throwing all the systems I had worked so hard on literally into large dumpsters outside. Our operational manuals, scheduling systems, forms, all gone! As much as I wanted to embrace the change, I was too distraught; besides, I still didn't know if I had a job.

While I feel that ABRA could have handled this acquisition much better (and they have gotten much better since), I had allowed myself to fall into a victim's mindset. ABRA let me stay on with them as a location manager for another seven months and while I never quite embraced the ABRA culture, I learned a tremendous amount of information that I can use today to help independently-owned collision shops improve their businesses. My experiences with ABRA, while quite difficult at times, proved to be a great learning experience for me, and would eventually guide me to a new fulfilling chapter of my life.

As I have seen in other markets around the world, once a platform acquisition takes place such as Bradshaw's, it starts a domino effect. Within a year, ABRA acquired several more stores, and soon after another large collision repair consolidator, Service King, purchased two more of Tennessee's largest independently-owned multi-shop operations (MSOs). Middle Tennessee by 2014 had more consolidator-owned body shops than independently owned. Many of those that had not been purchased yet had at least been approached to sell. Panic and fear had set in. Collision owners' belief systems were manipulated through fear to conclude that if they didn't sell, they would eventually be put out of business. Sadly, some of this manipulation was indeed self-imposed, comparing themselves to retailers competing with the almighty Walmart effect. It wasn't just going on in Tennessee either. The entire United States was experiencing the same thing in metro statistical areas that best met the platform growth strategy of the giant MSO consolidators. By this same time, Denver, for example, had all four of the largest MSOs operating in its market. ABRA, Service King, Boyd/Gerber, and Caliber were in a race to each hit the one billion sales mark first!

The effects of consolidation were profound. Not just from the standpoint of the body shop owners, but also the various businesses that supply them. It wasn't enough that paint and body supply jobbers were concerned about their best customers being bought out, their industry segment was also under consolidation by larger suppliers. I think it would be fair to say that consolidation is a natural occurrence. It's a simple concept. If you build a better business operating model, one that allows for rapid growth, and then you go for it, you would expect to grow. I don't hate big business; I admire what they have accomplished in many respects. I don't necessarily agree with all the values—and vision—of some of the industry giants, but do believe that if smaller businesses would pay attention to the factors that allow consolidators to grow, it could greatly benefit them.

Despite having been in the collision industry for nearly thirty years, it wasn't until this point in my life that I truly discovered my mission in life. The creation of Elite Body Shop Solutions and this book are an outcome of this mission to help business owners discover for themselves the amazing power that they possess. This power can be accessed by first challenging all the defeating beliefs that most of us have been conditioned to accept as our reality. Much of this book discusses the actual actions taken by real collision repairers who have allowed themselves to overcome the many challenges our industry faces and create amazing businesses and fulfilling lives for those who operate these businesses. This book is a celebration of the brave, independent entrepreneurs who continually challenge the status quo, and embrace the challenges instead of becoming victims.

Chapter 1

● ● ●

SECRET ONE – BUSTING OLD BELIEFS

*"Whether you think you can or
think you can't, you're right!"*

— HENRY FORD

THE VICTIM'S MINDSET

A body shop owner in Trenton, New Jersey, recently said to me, "Well Dave, all this stuff you're telling us about the industry all sounds real and good, and it might just work like you say in Tennessee, but it just don't work that way here in Jersey!"

These are the kind of excuses I hear from all parts of the United States, and even abroad. "Dave, you just don't understand what things are like for me; you see I have these problems with..." and the list goes on and on. It's like all the shop owners and managers (shop leaders) I meet think they have a rare, special problem that no one else would understand. I find these types of statements somewhat insulting. The very people I love and admire most in this industry have a terrible, horrible problem, and it is not external like whether an insurance company will pay for certain aspects of the repair. The real issue isn't how many big body shop companies have moved into town recently and are cutting their prices. These are indeed challenges, but to find the root of this horrible, terrible problem, all a person has to do is look in the mirror!

What I am going to share with you in the following chapters will not make a profound difference in your life unless you are first willing to take an honest look at yourself. The victim's mindset or what I like to refer to as entering the "victim zone," is a condition that we often enter unconsciously. While working for ABRA Auto Body and Glass in 2012, I too entered this zone whenever it felt like the outcomes expected of me were unrealistic, or the tasks required were outside of my comfort zone. I would tell myself things like, "Whoever came up with this budget clearly doesn't understand the Tennessee market," and then I would just give up. "Why even try when the cards are always stacked against me?"

Due to all the challenges our industry faces today, I totally understand why minds and actions can so easily drift into the victim zone. The trick to getting out of the victim zone is to take full accountability for yourself and your conditions—to quit blaming everyone else for your problems, and begin challenging your current belief system. The negativity that is experienced in the victim zone sets up a vicious cycle. When bad things happen, it then confirms and strengthens your faulty beliefs and your need to be right, which leads you to stay in your comfortable victim zone. This causes you to avoid making the necessary changes to improve your situation, and more bad things continue to happen.

One of the biggest contributors keeping us caught in the "doom loop" is the people we associate with. I mean who doesn't want to get together and complain about the insurance industry? This is what far too many industry gatherings sound like:

Jeff: Hey Bob, I was at a Mike Anderson seminar last week. He said we should be performing diagnostic scanning on cars during the initial inspection and again after the repairs are completed.

Bob: Yeah, I heard about that. Too bad the insurance companies won't pay for it.

Fred: Yeah, who is supposed to be paying for all this stuff the insurance companies are refusing to pay for anyway? I can't keep taking it in the shorts on every job and expect to stay in business!

Bob: I hear ya. With all these consolidator shops moving into town and suppressing our labor rates, scanning cars will be the least of our worries. Besides, I am sure Mike Anderson was only talking about scanning the cars coming out in the future. When I see a check engine light on, I'll send it to the dealer so I can make sure the insurance company will pay me plus mark up.

Jeff: You guys are probably right. Who can afford a scan tool these days anyway?

What Jeff, Bob and Fred need is a swift kick in the back end! When good people are in the victim zone and they get together, it quickly becomes a good old-fashioned gripe session. These conversations do nothing more than speed up the doom loop, helping to reinforce your faulty beliefs. This keeps you from changing to better behaviors, causing the bad things to happen continually. If you want to be a winner, you must hang out with other winners. Winners don't sit around and complain about how bad everything is. Instead, they avoid negative people and constantly challenge the things others are telling them as the absolute truth. They even challenge some of the things they were brought up to believe themselves. Challenging your beliefs does not make you wishy-washy; it makes you wise. What makes you wishy-washy is when you're not in alignment with your values.

> *"Challenging your beliefs does not make you wishy-washy, it makes you wise."*

Even if some of the things our three friends said are true, they are probably only partially true. They most likely also say things like, "Well, I can't schedule cars into my shop on Wednesdays.

The insurance company only allows me to bring cars in on Mondays so they don't have to pay for rental cars on the weekends!" Maybe some of you are guilty of this one? How about, "They [the insurance companies] only allow me to take in customers' cars when all of the parts have arrived first."

For those of you who read the previous paragraph and are bewildered because you also believe these statements to be true, let me digress momentarily to debunk these beliefs. Yes, of course, we have all had insurance adjusters tell us they would prefer that damaged vehicles come in on Mondays. They've also said they want us to pre-order all the parts off the estimate that was written without first disassembling the vehicle. The people who tell you this kind of nonsense are completely clueless to how production works. Bringing all the cars in for the week on Monday causes endless problems for any production system, including poor customer service and bottlenecks in the paint department. Furthermore, it creates such chaos in the shop that most of the cars you bring in on Monday don't get started until later in the week. The insurance person who asked you to do this—thinking it will save money on a rental car—is ridiculous and wrong because the vehicles probably aren't going to go home by Friday and a rental is going to be needed over the weekend anyway! People who truly understand how production works know that you need to have cars coming in every day of the week to create optimum flow in all departments.

How about the belief that pre-ordering parts will make your cycle time faster? This belief would probably be true if not for one factor. We usually write incomplete estimates first. I have performed some mini time studies based on this belief. What

I've found is that the only time pre-ordering helps is when you can perform an accurate repair appraisal that usually includes disassembling the damaged vehicle. What many of the shops in this country do is literal insanity. They write an estimate without being able to see all the damage and then order the parts that they *guess* are needed. Some shops even order parts based off an insurance company written estimate, having never even inspected the damage first. The well-meaning insurance appraiser tells the shop, "Here's the estimate, go ahead and get the parts coming. I will set up the rental for Monday. Let me know if you need anything else."

America's greatest body shops and the fastest shops in the world with cycle times, averaging two to four days keys-to-key, would never in a million years try to operate with this antiquated thinking. However, most shops in this country still believe in this nonsense. Great shops do one of two things: They either perform minor, temporary disassembly during an estimate appointment to identify all the damage up front and only then pre-order parts; or they wait until the vehicle arrives for a repair appointment to perform a thorough disassembly and "blueprint" prior to ordering parts. It may seem counterintuitive because of how we have been conditioned, but pre-ordering parts without a proper repair plan creates a multitude of wasteful activities that can lead to worse cycle times. Multiple parts orders, returns, extra manpower, stress, and chaos are just some of the problems that this thinking can cause, not to mention the potential strain it often puts on vendor relationships.

You will notice when people are in the victim zone they tend to speak in absolutes about their beliefs. They use words like never, only and always. These are a sign of a "closed" mind and someone stuck in, you guessed it, the victim zone! I don't mind when a person with strong morals or values speaks in absolutes because that shows conviction. Again, beliefs and values are often two different things. When you catch yourself saying things like, "Our insurance partners <u>only</u> allow us to bring cars in on Mondays," or "The customers in our community are <u>always</u> too busy for proper communication," it's time to check in with yourself to make sure you are not stuck in the victim zone!

Winners are faced with many of the same challenges as losers; however, only winners tend to look at challenges as opportunities. Being successful has more to do with how you think and perceive situations than it does with your current circumstances. As I have said many times before, right now is a great time to be in the collision repair business for those with the right mindset.

We talked to Dan Stander of Fix Auto Highlands Ranch in Littleton, Colorado, about these challenges and how they can also be viewed as opportunities. Dan grew up in the auto body business. The third-generation body shop operator recalls sweeping floors as a young boy in his grandfather's body shop in Englewood, Colorado. His two uncles also owned body shops and his father was repairing cars out of his home garage.

Suffice to say, his family has been in this business for as long as he can remember. After working with another shop for a brief time, Dan's father and mother, Jerry and Bernie, opened their shop, Jerry Stander's Auto Body. Except for a few side jobs growing up, Dan has always worked at his family's body shop, which is located in the heavily consolidated Denver area. Fast forward to January of 2011; Jerry and Bernie became founding members of Fix Auto USA and began to operate Fix Auto Highlands Ranch.

Dan Stander, Fix Auto Highlands Ranch

CASE STUDY: DAN STANDER – FIX AUTO HIGHLANDS RANCH

I remember when ABRA moved into town (approximately twenty years ago). In Colorado, the market was very pro-independent and nobody gave them much thought. But, as we know now, they were and still are a game-changer.

I don't think there's anything spectacular or different about what ABRA and the other consolidators are doing inside their shops. It's what they are doing outside their shops. These consolidators are coming into the markets and taking a huge market share, buying up shops and building new shops.

Some shops think that they can't stay in business with those darn consolidators coming in. That is totally wrong. There are a ton of opportunities created by consolidation. Part of the opportunity is really knowing what is going on in the market with consolidation.

One of the benefits the consolidators have is buying power. We call it "breaking the ceiling." In the past, if someone received a ten or twenty percent discount on paint, that was considered great. Now, the consolidators come to market and ask for a thirty, forty, or even fifty percent discount. That has broken the ceiling for us to negotiate better discounts.

Although they're taking business away from everybody, it's important to figure out how to fix that, how to do better for your employees, your business, and your customers. There is always opportunity in something that is negative. Sometimes, it's just fighting it. It's also changing culture, although culture can be very difficult to change.

Culture needs to come from top management in the shop and I think this is where an independent shop can struggle. I think business coaches are very important, too. Sometimes, bringing an independent third-party into your business can be very beneficial and help our shops become better.

In my opinion, if you're in a market that is consolidating, you have to figure out how to do things differently. If you can do it on your own, God bless you. For me and a lot of other folks

I know, it takes a group of people to be able to tackle these problems and compete against the consolidators.

Stander shares information in Chapter 6 about his involvement in ASA Colorado, as well as the importance of peer groups.

FEAR

Fear is what we experience when we are threatened—a natural response that may have been necessary back in the old days when we were surrounded by predators of the saber-toothed variety. Fear kept us from becoming some creature's lunch! In modern times, we still experience fear all the time, but it is only truly life-threatening on rare occasions. We still feel the same saber-toothed level of fear during non-life threatening circumstances such as public speaking, being made to look unintelligent, and most frequently, when we challenge the status quo. We worry too much about what others think of us! The problem with fear is that modern man doesn't know how to use it as a tool. Fear can be a decent motivator, but unfortunately, it usually becomes debilitating. We allow fear to run our lives instead of using it to our advantage.

Fear is a huge subject, but for the sake of what we are discussing, I will point out how fear affects our belief systems. Fear of the unknown, its cousin—the fear of change—and the almighty fear of *what other people think of us* are what keeps people small and feeling insignificant. Life has so much to offer. Instead, we allow fear to keep us from achieving the very life that our creator intended us to have. We live unconscious lives, never realizing how the fears we have accumulated over the years have affected us. We often accept the beliefs of others because we care too much about what they think, instead of caring more about being who we truly are. This is what is referred to as social conditioning, or what I like to call social oppression. Because people fear moving out of their comfort zones, they stay stagnant, and along the way, they justify that it is okay to be mediocre.

Society has taught us for many years that we need to go to college, get a good job, and raise a family with 1.87 kids. Schools, churches, our family and friends have taken years, and years of these beliefs, and with good intention, thrust them upon you. Without question, many of you have accepted these beliefs as your truth, whether right or wrong. Sadly, much of what people believe is based on inaccurate information. So how do you know what I am telling you is true? I am not asking you to believe me; I only hope you consider my advice from years of discovering what is best for collision repairers. I am only encouraging you to think differently before accepting everything people tell you as the truth—especially if it is coming from the insurance industry (just kidding).

Whenever you begin to move out of your comfort zone, your friends might kindly remind you that they care about you, so they feel obligated to tell you that your ideas and your reckless actions will likely fail! They will try to pull you back into your comfort zone, and you probably won't want to disappoint them, so you listen. After all, we all feel like we need to belong to a tribe.

You'll commonly hear statements like: "Be more like us!" "Rich people take advantage of others to gain their wealth." "You need to go to college, earn a degree, and become a doctor; why would you ever want to be an entrepreneur?" "Too much risk! You'll never make it!"

The people giving this advice often feel they are doing you a favor, but actually they need to be right, to protect their beliefs and egos. If you succeed and achieve your dreams, that would make them wrong, and nobody wants to be wrong! Choose your tribe wisely if you want to be a winner.

"Choose your tribe wisely if you want to be a winner."

Consider for a moment the effect that fear has had on our industry's consolidation by larger collision businesses. I have never heard a person from one of the big companies say, with an evil laugh (muah ha, ha), "I will feed on the fears of the independent repair community and take over the whole industry." However, this fear is indeed feeding right into their advantage. Consolidators being evil is not what's causing the massive consolidation we have experienced over the past few years. It is our own lack of self-confidence as independent repairers, and the fear that we won't be able to survive long-term, that makes many shop owners want to sell while they still can. Ironically, it is not only the big four consolidators that have benefitted from shop owners being caught in the victim zone. There are a handful of independently-owned collision repair businesses that are finding substantial growth—businesses that, of course, refuse to fall victim to the status quo.

Brad Mewes, principal of Supplement, helps businesses increase their value through mergers and acquisitions. His company provides strategic and financial advisory services, with a focus on the automotive aftermarket worldwide. Having grown up working in his family's auto body shop, Brad has a hands-on perspective about the industry. He shared some thoughts on consolidation and the future for independents.

Since the beginning of 2012, the industry has gone through an aggressive period of consolidation. Large companies, backed by Wall Street investment funds, have grown aggressively, primarily by purchasing smaller organizations. Some of these smaller organizations exceeded $100 million in sales. Others, only a few million in sales.

The large consolidators all started in a small way. Caliber was founded by a group of shop owners in Southern California. Boyd, the parent company of Gerber in the U.S., started as a single location in Winnipeg, Manitoba. Service King started as a single location in Dallas, Texas. ABRA started as a single location in Fridley, Minnesota. All of these founders saw an opportunity to do things differently in an industry defined by the status quo. Growth requires doing things differently. What worked in the past twenty years will not work in the next five. I grew up in my family's collision repair business and have seen the changes firsthand. I ultimately left the family business for one reason—to help other business owners grow and expand, and to help a new generation of shop owners achieve the same success that the large consolidators have achieved to date.

Now is actually one of the best times ever to grow your auto body business. The industry is more competitive and more difficult than it has ever been. There are a lot of peo-ple looking to retire. There are a lot of people frustrated. That creates opportunity.

The large consolidators already did the hard work. Insurers are comfortable with multi-unit operators. Technology makes it easier than ever before to run multiple locations. Vendors are very excited to work with businesses that have multiple locations. Even financing an acquisition in the auto body space has become easier as a result of consolidation.

It may sound counterintuitive but now really is one of the best times ever to expand your business, whether that be expanding your current location, buying just one more location, or even one hundred more locations!

DEALING WITH FEAR IN A PRODUCTIVE WAY

Because of many years of social conditioning with unfounded fears deeply engrained, you cannot simply snap your fingers and expect to overcome it all. It takes practice. Like any skill to be mastered, winners will practice observing their own behaviors, learning to make the unconscious decisions they make, con-scious. Awareness is where to start. When you can learn to catch yourself being a victim, or making justifications in order to keep yourself inside of your comfort zone, you'll become more aware of what is going on in your mind. People who have learned aware-ness, recognize fear as a positive thing. For example, whenever I feel fear creeping up into my body, I use it as a reminder that my fear is an amazing opportunity to grow and reach my potential.

As I mentioned earlier, winners hang out with winners. Even with a great mindset, it can be quite challenging to stay positive if you have a lot of negative, small-minded people around you all the time. If you are serious about being a winner, you may have to either fire some of your friends, make a conscious decision to hang out with them less, or find new ones. This may sound harsh, but most successful people know that you are probably like the five people you spend the majority of your time with!

CHAPTER 1 TAKEAWAYS

* Be accountable for yourself and your circumstances; avoid the "victim zone!"
* Hang out with winners.
* Challenge your beliefs—it does not make you "wishy-washy."
* Look at challenges as opportunities that can give you an edge.
* Be careful not to fall into the status quo trap.
* Practice and learn to become aware of your body's signals and then face your fears.
* Get comfortable being "uncomfortable."
* Remember that the magic always happens outside of your comfort zone.

Chapter 2

• • •

SECRET TWO – OVERCOMING CHALLENGES OF THE FAMILY-OPERATED BUSINESS

"We cannot solve our problems with the same thinking we used when we created them."

— ALBERT EINSTEIN

I often tell people that my first business, Luehr's Auto Body, was my ultimate education because from the standpoint of learning from failure, I learned a lot! Don't get me wrong, I did a lot of things correctly and was very proud of my accomplishments, but looking back, wow, I had a lot to learn about running a family business! I can legitimately call it a family-run business because my first wife worked with me as the office manager— at least until we divorced a couple of years later. My younger brother also worked for me for a while, until I had to fire him. My brother and I laugh about it today, but at the time, it was really challenging to work with family. The pressures of living with someone that you also work with all day long can be quite a challenge and I admire those who make their marriages, their families, and their businesses all work together.

You may wonder why I am including a chapter on family-owned businesses in this book. There are a couple of reasons. First, I have spent most my life working in family-owned and operated businesses and consider myself an expert on the subject. Second, ninety percent of businesses in America are considered a family business per the U.S Census Bureau. A family-operated business would be best defined as any business with two or more family members involved. While many of us never give the matter a second thought, these types of companies tend to include a layer of complication that has been known to be challenging. While I see tremendous benefits to the family-operated business, lack of awareness of these challenges can have devastating consequences to both the business, its employees, and most importantly, the family.

I worked for and consulted with several family-owned businesses over the last couple of decades and noticed a similar trend among those I assisted. I am generalizing this a bit because we know that there are many women in the industry too, but the following scenario seems to be most prevalent.

The father, usually a Baby Boomer, founded the company many years ago and grew up with the work ethic and leadership style learned from the Industrial Age. The second generation, a Gen "X" or Gen "Y" son, often does not have the same work ethic or views on how to lead people as dear old Dad. These businesses were built on the backs of the founders through sheer hard work, strong values, and a 'crack the whip' leadership style that worked well for them in the past. But here is the rub. The same leadership style that made these founders successful is now viewed by the modern workforce as corrosive, and in many cases demotivating. The second and sometimes third generations that are now second in command to the current owner, find themselves at odds with their fathers on how to lead their teams and deal with all the operational day-to-day challenges.

It is not only the younger generation that is frustrated with these family dynamics, but also the founders or current owners. Because they have such strong values around work ethics, they often see their children as incapable of running the operation. In some cases, I have found this view to be true, but not always. Often, the sons or daughters do not possess the work ethic, and in a few cases, lack the desire to run the family business effectively. However, I have seen an equal-size percentage of the younger generation who are more than capable of taking it over and running it successfully, but getting dear old Dad to agree can be a challenge. What he fails to recognize is that the Industrial Age has long since passed, and if modern leadership and operational systems are embraced, the company would get back on track to super success! This can be a hard pill to swallow for the founders because it means they would have to challenge their long-held beliefs about how a body shop should be operated.

A poorly-operated collision repair shop can be very tough for the employees too. Communication is typically poor at body shops to begin with, and some family-owned shops can be even worse. I was doing some consulting work with the owner of a good-sized shop in rural Tennessee. I interviewed the shop manager who was a great guy. You could tell he knew a lot about the collision repair industry, and he had been working for my client's shop for nearly twenty years. He began complaining to me that the gal at the front desk wasn't doing her job. He also said that the parts and production manager never mirror-matched parts and the estimators didn't update customers. I asked him, "Well when you discussed this gap in performance with these individuals, what did they have to say for themselves?"

He said, "Well… uh, I have never talked to them about it." I asked, "Why not, aren't you the shop manager?" He then explained to me that the receptionist is the owner's daughter, her husband is the parts and production manager, and the estimator, who had just literally returned from drug and alcohol rehab, is their cousin. As it turned out, the manager, the guy who is supposed to hold everybody accountable, was almost the only person in the shop that wasn't related to the owner!

Communication is essential to a successful operation, and when a family is involved, it is crucial to discuss the "elephant in the room" even when it feels uncomfortable. Safety is the key to creating a culture where people communicate well, and only organizations that do this will be able to come close to achieving their potential success. Safety means that employees, at all levels, feel comfortable discussing topics that may be hindering them to perform their best work. The best leaders consciously engage in conversations with the team and family to bring important conversations out on the table without people fearing repercussions.

It takes guts to embark on building a healthy culture, and it also takes time. For businesses that are new to working on improving communication, you must be cognizant that for many employees it will take a while for them to trust leadership and each other enough to talk openly. Don't be discouraged as a leader if people take time to open up to you, as many workers in the collision repair industry have never been exposed to a truly healthy culture. Conduct regular improvement meetings, initiate one-on-one coaching sessions, and always follow through on promises made during these discussions or people won't take leadership seriously.

Communication skills are one of the most important skills a person can possess. Not only is it critical to possess them as a leader, but you must also have these skills as a member of the family. Only on rare occasions have the families I've worked with been able to figure out how to respectfully and openly speak to each other. As a result, these businesses have all suffered greatly. There are very specific skills that can be learned to improve your communication and give you the confidence to say what needs to be said without upsetting everyone in the process. A book that has changed my life in many ways, both professionally and personally, is called "Crucial Conversations," by the authors Grenny, Patterson, Switzler, and McMillan. It is a book based on behavioral science and provides proven strategies that can improve your life and the lives of everyone around you.

The good news is that despite the challenges involved, a family-operated business can offer a tremendously inviting culture to many workers. This culture can translate into a positive customer experience that I doubt could be consistently duplicated by a large corporate collision business. I believe that most people still prefer to do business with locally-owned, family companies whenever it is convenient to do so. I recommend that family-owned shops exploit the advantages they have to create a tremendous customer experience in every way possible. I have worked as an employee for both well-run and not so well-run family businesses. I have also worked for large corporations, and I must say that I prefer working for a well-run family business. I am positive many others feel the same way. The key here is "well-run." Nobody wants to work in some of the family dysfunction that is still extremely prevalent in our industry today!

When you add the many new challenges collision repairers are faced with these days, it is no wonder that industry consolidation has run rampant in the past few years as many founders face the aforementioned generational dilemma. Although I am happy for those owners who have built an amazing business, and then sold it for their retirement nest-egg, I think it is a shame for those who felt they needed to exit due to frustration with the industry, and with their kids. What many of them didn't realize was that they might have missed an incredible opportunity to perpetuate the family business into an even better one with their very own kids at the helm!

For those shops that currently face generational challenges, I encourage you to come together through enhanced communication. Families must learn to talk through these misunderstandings brought on by different generational value systems. Learn new skills! The skills in this book are a great place to start—particularly when it comes to leadership. The workforce that exists in shops these days is much different than when many businesses were first founded. It requires a pull "servant" style of leadership as opposed to the push "boss" style from the old days.

For family businesses that can embrace the challenges of the modern age, I strongly believe there is an excellent opportunity for prosperity. Don't underestimate the number of people who still prefer doing business with a family-owned, local company.

> *"Don't underestimate the number of people who still prefer doing business with a family-owned, local company."*

One of these family businesses is King Collision Centers in Massachusetts, which includes two locations in Pembroke and Plymouth. Bruce King founded the company in 1983 after his father encouraged him to go into the collision repair industry. His son Chris joined the family business while still in high school and took it over in 2013. Although the company has grown and changed in many ways since then, Chris said the primary focus is still the same: doing what is necessary to create "customers for life."

Bruce and Chris King, King Collision Centers

CASE STUDY: THE KINGS – KING COLLISION CENTERS
Bruce

I went to a big vocational school to learn collision repair. In ninth grade, I was having a tough time at school and my dad suggested I take auto body and we would open a business together. By the time I finished school, he was the general manager of the shop he was working at and it would have been foolish for him to start a business with me.

I went into the insurance appraisal business and decided to start my own company representing insurance companies. It was great education because I learned from the insurance industry what matters to them, and how to get paid for what you are doing. Not only did it afford me the opportunity to earn the income to build my first shop five years later, but it also gave me entrance into every single one of my future competitors and see how they were operating their businesses. It was a golden opportunity to learn more in a short period of time than I could learn in twenty-five years owning and operating a shop.

I've always said, "The best game in town is the other guy's game because he is never expecting you to play it."

I found over the years that it always boils down to one thing—customer service. There is only one person who comes into the shop who is indispensable. It's not the technicians or the production people, and it's not me. It's the customer. Most businesses just don't understand it's not about them. All you have to do is ask the customer what he wants. That's the key.

When my son, Chris, was going through a tough time in tenth grade, he came to work for me. He started on the lowest rung on the totem pole and began sweeping floors after school, cleaning the shop and emptied the trash. Eventually, he became a detailer and cleaned cars.

When you work with your kids, you are able to develop your children's business education and acumen. You are teaching them things that they are not going to learn at a course. It gives you an opportunity to spend time with them and help them develop their people skills and understand what it takes to own and operate a business. It's not a nine-to-five job. Another benefit is that you develop great trust between you and your child. I would tell Chris, "At work, I'm your boss, at home I'm your dad." You end up with a dual relationship.

What I have found is that my children have come to respect me more because they understand what it took and what I went through daily to feed, clothe and shelter them. I also cared very much about our employees. Their families were counting on my decisions for their livelihood and I took that responsibility extremely seriously. Now my kids understand that too. They are very focused on the employees and that's why we have great staff. There is virtually no turnover. Some have been with us more than thirty years. It's like a family. I never wanted a business; I wanted a cult—something so cool going on inside the business that it vibrates out into the middle of the street.

Since my son Chris has taken over, he has made some changes. By and large, he has done an awesome job. There are a few things that he has changed that I would have done differently, but it's not my business anymore. I might give him advice and tell him how I would address something. Then I say, "Prove me right or wrong and be happy."

When I first left school, I worked at the same company as my dad, and it was hard. Fathers tend to be more demanding and expect more from their children than the other employees. My father was like that with me and there was a time when I was the same with Chris.

For those in a similar situation considering retiring, my advice is for the current owner to figure out what he really wants. If you tell your kids that you want to retire, then you better mean what you say. Too many guys say they want to retire, but they don't have anything else to do. It's important to find something to do outside of work and with your time that you care about and you can put that same kind of focus and energy into so you're not sitting around being bored. I'm still working on that.

Then talk to your kids and let them know your plan; together you can map out how things are going to be structured. There are a lot of financial considerations. An attorney or a third-party can help guide you through the process. It's incumbent on both the parent and child to sit down and crunch the numbers to understand what is reasonable. Above all, understand that if you've trained your child correctly, don't get upset when he or she is ready to be the boss. If the current owner is going to sell the business, or have it taken over by one or more of the children, don't lose sight of the fact that they are your children and you love them. In real life, family is more important than anything.

Chris
Working with family can be very rewarding and comforting most times. I truly feel that everyone in my company is part of my family, particularly those who have worked here for many years. We have fifty employees at our two locations in Pembroke and Plymouth. When you, your family and your team are in sync and working toward the same vision and goals, I think nothing can get in your way or prevent you from succeeding.

However, it can be challenging to separate work time from family time and not let the two impact decisions that need to be made for your business or family. Working with my dad was very educational, but could also be extremely challenging at times. He was an extremely passionate, aggressive and tough business owner. I learned a lot from him—what to do and not to do. We are similar in many ways, sharing a similar passion, pride and goals for the business, but we are different as well, especially coming from two generations.

I found my dad had a different emotional connection to the business than I did. Like most founders, he put a lot of effort into building the business. There are different risks and issues associated with building a company until it achieves financial stability and is able to stand on its own. Many businesses, particularly those in the collision repair industry, are started without much if any financial backing. When everything is on the line, it becomes a major concern and failure is not an option. With this pressure, it fuels the owner to operate the business 24/7 and put it above anything else, while riding the new proprietorship wave.

Although I think the business is still equally important to the founder as to the next generation, the founder never stops viewing the business like a young child of sorts. The founder protects and is emotionally attached to the business literally like it's a child.

As a second-generation owner, I haven't had to deal with these same concerns. I am still emotionally attached but in a much different way—more of a business-like relationship. I view the business as a fictitious person who, although is not a living breathing human, is always the most important person and topic in all conversations. The needs of the entity always come first. The reality is that if we always protect and nurture the business, it will provide for all of us.

My dad's generation grew up in a very low technological world. There was a lack of technology in tooling, office equipment, communication tools, environmental improvement and training. Technology now shapes our world and industry much differently, and very quickly—at times too quick. This allows us to operate professional businesses with procedures and structure.

When my dad was in the collision repair industry, it was very much a technician-owned and operated industry. Many techs stopped working for someone else and opened collision repair businesses. Some of these moves where good and they *made it, but others probably should have stayed working for someone else because they did not help the industry in a positive manner nor did they bring value to the customer and the communities they were serving.*

My advice to others in a family business is to differentiate your goals and figure out why you are in the collision repair business in the first place. I found it's very helpful to have a good group of friends and people you can talk with. Find people inside and outside of the industry that you can share ideas and discuss your challenges with and seek advice from. Surround yourself with people you truly like and enjoy spending a lot of time with on a daily basis who want to accomplish the same goals and visions you are inspired by.

CHAPTER 2 TAKEAWAYS

* It is essential to learn modern leadership skills.
* Differing generational values should be discussed and embraced.
* Learn communication skills and always talk about the "elephant in the room" no matter how difficult it is.
* Make your business a safe place to communicate openly.
* Exploit the uniqueness and benefits of being a family-owned business.

Chapter 3

● ● ●

SECRET THREE – BUILDING A SUSTAINABLE BUSINESS MODEL

*"It is not enough to do your best; you must
know what to do, and then do your best."*

– W. Edwards Deming

America's greatest body shops are taking back control of their businesses. I am not trying to take anything away from hair salons, but we can't continue operating like a hair salon that rents out space to an entrepreneurial staff, and then lets the techs determine the success or failure of the business. There is too much at stake these days. With all the complexities with today's collision repair industry, business owners can no longer afford to abdicate all of the operational complexities to their teams without first having great systems in place. Then they can take ownership to ensure that the systems are consistently and correctly being used.

I have fond memories of my days as a "firefighter." Some nightmares too. Not a firefighter in the real sense, but by God I could sure put out some fires on a busy Friday afternoon! I would drive from Salem, Oregon to Portland two times on a Friday to pick up parts that we forgot to order, so we could get those cars to go home on time and still manage to meet payroll. Back in the '80s and '90s, many of us prided ourselves on how well we held together during the constant chaos that was our "normal" life in the body shop. It's no wonder that only a few of us had multiple locations back then; we would have killed ourselves trying to manage more than one! Sadly, many of the shops in our country still operate this way thirty years later, and we have stress and health issues as a result.

I think one of the greatest business books I have read was *The E-Myth: Why Most Small Businesses Don't Work and What to Do About It* by Michael Gerber. Even though the original version of *E-Myth* came out nearly three decades ago, the material could not be more relevant than it is right now to our industry. If you haven't read it, I would definitely add it to your reading list soon. It explains the dynamics that occur from the time a technician decides to become a business owner, through the stages of growth before a business reaches maturity. I feel where most collision repair leaders get it wrong is when it comes to building a sustainable model.

Most shop owners do not seem to build a business model that will operate efficiently, especially when they decide to become a multi-store operation (MSO). Every successful business should always be built with the vision to sell or grow like it was a franchise model even if the owner doesn't want to sell it or franchise it. Most of us don't do this well with one location, let alone several. I frequently meet frustrated owners who are excellent in their own mind at running two or three locations, but once they grow beyond that level, the whole operation falls apart. The skill set required to operate a sizable MSO properly is very different than those running a single store or small MSO.

One thing MSO consolidators have done very well recently is to build an operational model that allows for rapid growth. Many can remember the failed and mediocre attempts at industry consolidation by several of America's largest players in the early 2000s (and don't forget about the famous collapse of M2 Collision Care Centers in 2005). Since that time, key people at the big four MSOs, and even some of the smaller ones, have learned from these failures and went back to the drawing board. Take ABRA for example. I am impressed with the company's operating model that has become their cornerstone for success since they introduced an "Operational Excellence" program in 2007. Having created a better operational model has allowed for massive growth where it may not have been possible before without it. Their ABRA Playbook is just that, their "playbook" and they use it every day as a foundation to create a consistent and repeatable experience for employees and customers alike, regardless of which location you visit.

Is the ABRA Playbook better than Service King's, Caliber's, or Gerber's? Some are slightly better than the others, but truth be told, it doesn't matter as much as you might think. What matters is that they *do* have written and well-communicated standards, plus, they know how to enforce them. Don't obsess about getting your hands on some operational magic by stealing the

ABRA Playbook; the real magic is in how you use the standards once you have them in place!

"You can't improve a system absent of standards."

One of the most important fundamentals to continuously improving and growing a business is to understand what the standards are first. This means everyone in the organization must have a clear idea of what is expected. You have most likely heard the phrase: "You can't improve what you don't measure." Well, you also can't improve a system absent of standards because without first establishing a standard, how are you going to measure it? What are you going to measure it against? Nothing? If you are a frustrated body shop owner or manager that is at your wit's end, there is a good chance it is because your team doesn't know what is expected of them! Is accountability an issue at your business? It may be because there is no standard in place, and therefore, no accountability. A business without clear, written, and communicated standards is a petri dish of festering arbitrary opinions where nobody wins!

Here is an example of what I am talking about. As the boss, you have seen some bad communication scores from your customer satisfaction index (CSI) provider and it looks like Bob the estimator may not be doing his job. So you say, "Bob, I am getting some horrible CSI scores. You need to improve your communication with the customers!" Now Bob, being a thirty-year veteran of the industry says, "That is total nonsense. I talk to these people every day when they call. I consider myself an excellent communicator!"

You see this conversation is already headed down the drain because it is all arbitrary nonsense. Suppose you had a written standard in your playbook. Perhaps then your conversation would be more like this: "Bob, I just got a bad survey back from Mr. Jones. According to the management system, you only called him once during the entire repair cycle. You know that our 'written standard' is to contact our customers every two days proactively. Can you please explain what happened?" The conversation now has meaning and some "teeth" for successful improvement. When you have standards, it changes everything, including employee engagement and satisfaction.

During the acquisition transition in 2012, when Bradshaw Collision Centers became ABRA Auto Body and Glass, I found, quite surprisingly, that not everyone making the transition with me detested it as much as I did. In fact, some people were relieved. Over the course of the following year after the acquisition, there were many people who quit, but there were some good people who stayed too. One of those people was my friend Brandy Jeter. Brandy was one of my favorite people at Bradshaw's, and always someone you could count on to make things happen when asked. A year after I left ABRA, I spoke to her over the phone and asked her how things were going at ABRA. I was fully expecting to hear something that had mirrored my experience with the company, but instead received an unexpected lesson on culture. She said, "You know Dave, I actually like working for ABRA better than working for Bradshaw's." She continued, "Every day that I come to work, I know exactly what is expected of me, I love it here!" After the shock had worn off, I found an important lesson contained in Brandy's words. One of the most critical factors that make companies like ABRA successful, and one of the biggest missing factors keeping a majority of independently-owned shops small and frustrated, is having clearly defined standards and the ability to hold people accountable to follow them. It can greatly contribute to a winning culture.

While I am singing the praises of the consolidators' ability to use standards and processes to their advantage, many of America's greatest independent shops both understand and apply this same lesson; some do it even better than the consolidators. A real advantage you have as an independently-owned business, whether a single store or regional MSO, is your ability to make things happen quickly with continuous improvement efforts. It is nearly impossible for the big MSOs to do the same, and it is also difficult for them to travel as far down the path of advanced production methodologies as I have seen in some of America's greatest shops.

You can learn a lot from these shops, and when you combine great leadership and a great company culture with clearly defined standards, you will have a winning combination that will lead to a huge competitive advantage, regardless of competition.

So how do you come up with these standards? Most paint and body supply manufacturers can provide you with standard operating procedures (SOPs) that you can use for the physical repair of the vehicle. For the SOPs used in the administrative processes such as answering phones, checking in cars, quality control, blueprinting, etc., there are ways you can do it yourself or use a company like Elite Body Shop Solutions to help you through the process. You don't need a two-hundred-page SOP manual to get the job done. The massive manuals I created years ago usually end up as someone's doorstop! All you need is a simple workflow document that lays out the basics—a "playbook" that people will actually read and refer to as they are learning how to perform the steps in the system. I like to incorporate checklists and simple "standard work instruction" sheets (SWIs).

If you want to create a playbook yourself, just begin documenting the preferred way you envision the activities performed, starting from beginning to end. This includes when a prospective customer first calls or walks in the door, throughout the entire process until the customer picks up the finished automobile.

A mistake that some shop leaders make is that they go to the trouble of creating standards, yet no one seems to know what they are! Be advised: over-communicate this information every way you can! Hold meetings with your staff regularly to train, discuss and answer questions about the standards. Another way that standards get overlooked is because people don't enforce them as well as they should. Nobody likes being seen as a jerk, but if you don't say something immediately about deviations from the agreed upon standards, you and your "standards" just become another "flavor of the month" joke. The next time you walk by a car that has dirty parts sitting on a customer's expensive leather seats, for Pete's sake, remind the employee what the standard is!

How do you know your team understands the standards? One way is to ask them occasionally to tell you what they are. Another way is to give them a test. Here I go giving more credit to the consolidators, but these guys are great at it. They have access to a learning management system that provides training on all SOPs, and the employees are required to take a test to prove they were paying attention. As a smaller company, you do not need a fancy learning management system to do this; you can easily create ten to twenty test questions yourself. Don't believe for a minute that your people are properly trained until they can prove it.

Now that you have your written standards in place and your team knows what they are, it is important to provide feedback if and when your employees meet your expectations. America's greatest body shops audit their systems regularly and provide feedback. The best of the best, like those utilizing the Bodyshop Revolution model* use software to keep track of process mistakes during the repair process. Using this information, Bodyshop Revolution shops hold regular problem-solving team meetings to help eliminate problems from reoccurring. This form of deliberate practice provides immediate feedback that can be used to

---

* A Bodyshop Revolution shop will track "Murphys" (unexpected errors) under multiple criteria, enabling short-, medium- and long-term review of both the cause and effect of those Murphys in terms of lost production. Tracking in this manner reveals valuable data like vendor issues, as well as individual estimator and technician performance. The information gathered by Murphy tracking becomes the primary driver for ongoing improvement in the business, giving essential, unbiased, hard data that is used in performance reviews with both staff and suppliers. It is also essential when reviewing Murphy tracking reports to look carefully at the SOP manual, and identify where procedural changes can assist in eliminating a Murphy.

Nothing in a Bodyshop Revolution shop is left to chance or acted on by "intuition." A shop that is already performing at elite levels will only improve further by measuring and testing, and tracking of Murphys is essential to this.

Information provided by Neil Parr-Davies, Chief Operating Officer, Bodyshop Revolution

improve operations continually. Some of the bigger MSOs are outsourcing process inspections to companies that specialize in auditing. Again, don't think you have to be a huge company to audit your systems. It is super easy to create a simple checklist that is based on your standards and start inspecting. You have to inspect what you expect or it won't get done!

> **"You have to inspect what you expect or it won't get done!"**

Simplicity is also important when it comes to creating standards and playbooks. Keep in mind once more that we are trying to build a "franchise-like" sustainable and repeatable business model. If you want to grow into multiple locations, you cannot get away with over-complicated processes. The best processes are those that everyone can follow. If you are designing systems around the shop's superstar body man, you may not be creating a sustainable and repeatable model. The beauty of what some of America's greatest body shops have done is to create systems where ordinary people can consistently achieve extraordinary results. Great companies do attract great people but make no mistake, you don't need a bunch of superstars to get the job done if you have good systems and standards.

MEASURE CRITICAL STEPS

An important aspect of leadership that keeps teams engaged is to share key performance indicators (KPIs) that matter with them. Teams are far more engaged when you can turn work into a game. People will become disengaged when they don't know how their efforts are contributing to the success of the company.

The tricky part here is to be smart about what you are measuring. This is even more important if you are rewarding people using these numbers. Measuring and sharing numbers on outcome metrics like CSI scores may be important to keep track of, but can also be dangerous when the people accountable for the metrics don't have full control of the events that go into creating the outcome.

Rant warning! It really upsets me when I see shop leadership denying an estimator a bonus because one of the customers gave them a poor CSI survey that was linked to their paycheck bonus. Look, you have to do your best to take care of all of your customers, but we all know there are customers who are unreasonable regardless of our best attempts. A secret to a great company culture is to put your employees first. In order for them to properly care for your customers, you must make them a top priority! That may be contrary to everything you've been conditioned to believe, but if you don't treat your employees well and give them lousy outcome-based bonus plans, they are not going to take care of the customers as you might think! If you want to measure them and keep them engaged, try rewarding them based on completing the individual critical steps that create the future outcomes, such as CSI.

A critical step is any process step that has a large impact on an outcome. For example, if you proactively contact your customers regularly throughout the repair process, this contributes to the outcome—a happy customer. If you want to hold someone accountable in this circumstance or provide meaningful feedback against a known standard, measure how often that person is contacting and documenting communication. There really is full control over that!

Fourteen and a half years ago, Randy Sattler came to work at Rydell GM Auto Center in Grand Forks, North Dakota. He had no background in the body shop industry and started in the service department. After being promoted to manager of the collision shop two years later, he began working closely with the owner of the dealership to help build a successful body shop using specific processes. These included some of the ones implemented in December 2014 with the help of Bodyshop Revolution. Randy stresses the importance of setting up processes in a body shop and says that it not only helps with better cycle time, but it builds closer relationships with employees and ensures a better overall product.

Randy Sattler, Rydell Collision Center

CASE STUDY: RANDY SATTLER – RYDELL COLLISION CENTER

When you look at other shops across the United States and Canada that have good performance with cycle time and hours per day, I believe it's because they've developed processes that work for their shop in their part of the world.

If you consider all the technology that is coming down the road, if you don't have solid and specific repair processes in place, it is a very real possibility that good repair facilities will deliver cars that might not necessarily be fixed correctly and it could create a lot of negativity in our industry. I believe that good, solid processes allow shops to function more efficiently, have better performance, have confidence that vehicles are being repaired correctly and have happier employees overall. We've also found that they can help eliminate employee stress and anxiety.

When Bodyshop Revolution came into our world in 2014, it was a huge culture change. Prior to that, we tried many different stages and types of blueprinting and mirror matching of parts, etc. but we couldn't get our processes consistent to the point where we didn't have what we call "process evaporation." We'd implement a new process, it would work well for a couple of weeks, maybe even a few months, but as time passed, we would see this process evaporation and after a period of time, we seemed to fall back to our comfort level of doing things the old way.

What we found was we didn't have a good set of ground rules or a good solid outline to follow that allowed us to monitor these new processes and be able to follow up correctly when they seemed to fail. In many cases, we had good training and we knew what we wanted to accomplish, but we just always seemed to chase success.

Once we found and were trained on Bodyshop Revolution's Vehicle Damage Assessment (VDA) process, it was a HUGE change on how we assessed vehicle damage. We had to change our thinking on how important estimating the vehicle was, and how it affects the complete repair. We had to understand how important accuracy of the estimate really was and also the importance of how we visually map our vehicles, and ultimately, the biggest reality was how we needed to look at the value of our metal and paint technicians.

We all know that starts and stops in this industry are a given. With the VDA, our goal is to eliminate as many of these starts and stops as possible. We know we can't stop them all, but if we can get better at determining the why of these stops, we can get better with our repair performance. Any time a technician has to stop working on a vehicle, we consider that a fail the same way as if a customer up front comes to pick up a vehicle and notices something that isn't properly repaired. The culture for us became that we looked at our technicians as customers of the estimating process and that anytime they had to leave their six-foot repair circle—the area around the repair that they are working on—that it is a fail.

Once we had the VDA in place, our first true success and example or what we call continuous workflow was a Chevy Cobalt repair. This happened on a Wednesday; the vehicle was a front-end hit with nine and a half hours of total repair work, metal and paint time. The tech started on it after his morning coffee break, about 9:15 a.m. and we were able to call the customer a little after 4:30 in the afternoon and he was here at 5:30 picking up his vehicle. That was a huge win for us, and that one repair helped all of us understand what we were really trying to accomplish—continuous workflow on a vehicle.

Typically, in some shops they may have a different tech for each of the following: taking the car apart, fixing it, prepping it, refinishing it and putting it back together. For some shops, this works great; for us, it did not. We spent too much time going back and forth and too many hands touched the vehicle; we wanted to simplify this.

The benefits of continuous workflow are better cycle time and hours per day. I think your better-performing body shops that are in the DRP world understand the importance of performance. It gives the shop the ability to receive more cars from insurance companies, which creates continuous work for the shop. In this industry, I think insurance companies have accepted subpar performance and as shops get better with process and performance, insurance companies will want to work with these shops.

When we talk about continuous workflow, it means that after the technician gets a vehicle into his stall for repair, our goal is that he is working on that one vehicle from the time that he starts in the morning until he completes it or punches out for the day. We don't allow him to work on another vehicle until it moves to paint, then typically, we'll have that technician look at his next job and he might do some pre-staging, pull his parts, etc. Our cycle time for going through the paint booth is about fifty-two to fifty-three minutes with a gas catalytic robot. The vehicle is not on the paint side very long, so the repairing technician will get his repair back for reassembly typically in sixty to seventy-five minutes. We truly work at getting four hours a day on every car that we repair that has four or more repair or refinish hours.

The most important part of the puzzle is the employees here. It's fun and impressive to talk about how we've grown over the years, but the reality is what we're doing here is a byproduct of a commitment from not only management but also from the employees. They are the people who deserve the credit because they didn't give up. Change for people is very, very hard and I am forever indebted to the people who were there during these changes, and continue to understand that continuous improvement means continually changing and trying new things.

One of the most valuable lessons that we have learned through all this is when we decide to either change a process or implement a new one, we will include any staff that will be touched by the change. We will sit down and talk about what it is we want to change or try, explain the why... and then listen to what their thought process might be. They deserve the opportunity to express their concerns and know how the change or new process might affect them and possibly their paycheck.

Another important thing to remember is any process change or shop repair experimentation can never come at the cost *of the employees. We've always tried to take care of our employees and I think that is why they've stayed here, and are still as committed today to get better as they were when we started this journey. All of us are in it together and we are all committed!*

KNOW YOUR NUMBERS

In terms of building a sustainable collision repair business, there are few things more important than understanding and using financial metrics. Another commonality of America's greatest body shops is that these leaders use financial data daily to make business adjustments, which keeps them on track to meet their business goals. This is a proactive approach to driving a business, as opposed to many owners who occasionally review a financial statement, and usually only after the damage has already been done and it is too late to make corrections.

Accurate and timely financial reporting is a critical component of a successful business and few people understand this better than my friend, Steve Trapp, who is the North American Services Manager for Axalta Coating Systems. When I told Steve about this book, I was very excited that he offered to contribute some advice from his many years in the industry as a pioneer in the development of the financial standards that are used by our industry to this day.

In the early 1980s, Steve worked closely with the pioneering team that included Lirel Holt from Dawn Enterprises, Dennis Kiyohara and a team from 3M who had collaborated to create the coveted ARM$ manual and influential 3M ARM$

seminar series. The 3M ARM$ series created an early blueprint to unlocking the financial model for the collision repair industry. The company's message was eye-opening, yet simple. 3M's industry-icon instructors taught repairers how to get familiar with their costs on a per job basis, connecting with the sale on that job and then calculating a per job gross profit. This process was then called "job costing" and continues at the foundation of all body shop management systems today; it is a critical component to monitor for body shops that want to prosper. They were also advocates of "true cost of labor." This tracks the cost of wages, taxes, recruiting, training and benefits to track the true labor cost, which will help repairers understand the overall labor margin.

Courtesy of Steve Trapp – Axalta Coating Systems

Gross Profit
Sales $ – Costs $ = Gross Profit $

Gross Profit $ / Sales $ = Gross Profit %

Sales $200,000 – Costs $120,000 = Gross Profit $80,000

Gross Profit $80,000 / Sales $200,000 = 40% Gross Profit

Knowing the gross profit or gross margin in a department provides awareness to your effectiveness managing cost. It can then be used as a basis to get paid to achieve the desired margin. If your business is not making the proper margin, look to reduce costs or raise prices.

Sales Mix

Recently, with the focus on overall severity / average return on investment (ROI) by insurers, there has been an increased focus on repairing panels rather than replacing parts, so moving towards 30-20-10, which represents a ratio of thirty percent body / frame / mechanical and twenty percent paint and detail and ten percent paint and material. The result is a higher overall gross profit percentage on a lower average RO.

Target Sales Mix and Gross Profit

	Sales Mix	Gross Profit %	Weighted Profit
Body Labor	28%	62%	17.36%
Paint Labor	17.5%	65%	11.38%
Parts	39.3%	28.9%	11.36%
Paint & Material	10.2%	44%	4.49%
Sublet	5%	20%	1.00%
Total	**100%**		**45.59%**

Axalta's 2016 Year-End National Business Council Averages

For shops that are near capacity, REPLACING parts and optimizing gross profit per hour sold, coupled with parts profits, optimizes profit if you have maximized the labor hours available. That capacity issue should be short-lived today in top body shops, as they can add staff, shifts, time-saving equipment like gas catalytic arches and over the longer term add additional square footage or a location nearby ("Express Center" or centralized "Heavy Hit" location) to produce this volume quickly.

Managerial Ratios as Lead Indicator
America's greatest body shops realize that achieving top financial performance means keeping the proper balance between top line sales and production.

Top Line Sales: We have found that budgeting top line sales, tracking repair volume traffic by sources, and closing ratio can be great ways to ensure the work in-flow or customer demand with production capability. For example, with written estimate traffic of $400,000 times seventy-five percent closing ratio is $300,000 in sales. Improving the sales process and growing closing ratio by five percent to eighty percent would result in a $20,000 sales improvement. Once you optimize closing ratio, then the focus becomes using market research to improve marketing efforts that drive in more estimate traffic dollars.

Production: Once the job is sold, you have to produce it. Taking a $300,000 sales with fifty percent labor is $150,000 in labor sales / $50 per hour = 3,000 hours / 21 working days per month = 143 hours per day. To have a level flow of production, each department (scheduling, repair planning, body repair, paint, reassembly and delivery) has to produce 143 hours. This often means changing and rethinking processes. During this stage, we often refine the staffing model, facility utilization and other production drivers.

Key Financial Reports
Most top shops place the majority of their emphasis on the income statement, concentrating on the sales mix,

departmental cost and gross profit. The other areas of financial focus are:

Expenses: *When examining overhead, expenses as a percentage of sales can be improved by doing a comparison with other shops to draw out the ideas that drive their success.*

Balance Sheet: *All repairers obviously have a balance sheet, but MOST tend to focus only on the cash on hand, accounts receivable, accounts payable and basics of short-term and long-term assets and liabilities, as well as what the equity accounts contain. Top shops have added book-keepers, controllers or CFOs who understand liquidity ratios to help ensure compliance to loan covenants with bankers. The larger the debt, the more important this is.*

Cash Flow: *Top shops looking to expand have embraced cash flow, realizing that effective repair planning and pre-closing files (paper precedes the repair process) to speed closing of files at delivery, drives sales and reduces work in process (WIP) inventory cost. Top shops also realize that timely collection procedures drive cash on hand, as well as smart account receivable policies, which take advantage of prompt pay terms and extended terms to stretch cash.*

Daily Operating Controls (DOCs)
A tool we learned from the new-car dealer world is a daily operating control (DOC) sheet. Dealers utilized this because they learned that waiting until month-end to review financial performance is very reactive and slow to affect change. We have found that when shops know each day what their

current KPIs (Key Performance Indicators) are relative to monthly or annual goals, they are far more likely to take the necessary actions to meet those goals. Top shops use various methods to collect and measure this information. DOCs can include the use of reports generated from management systems, or push reports from third-party organizations, or can simply be created by the shop using an Excel spreadsheet. These KPIs usually include metrics such as sales, gross profit, work in process, CSI, etc. A key to the successful use of a DOC sheet is setting solid targets per KPI and having the manager run the reports and track them daily.

Determine Strategic Financial Direction

As top shops look at financial statements, they should strategically consider the next few years' focus for their businesses. Those shops choosing to grow through acquisition or deciding to sell must understand how their financial performance can affect the abilities to leverage potential deals.

Leverage success and grow: For those wanting to grow through acquisition, maintaining world-class facilities, having effective training and optimizing KPIs is crucial. Focusing on pre-closing files to close them faster, minimizing inventory and cutting work-in-process inventory are all ways to optimize working capital to reinvest in growth. Then it is advisable to optimize balance sheet performance to keep banking ratios (such as times interest earned or acid test ratios) in line, so the bank makes cash available for timely and smart acquisitions.

Prepare business to sell: Those considering selling the business will need to focus strongly on "bottom line" *financial performance, as many consolidator organizations will determine purchase offers based on multiples of EBITDA (Earnings Before Interest, Taxes, Depreciation, Amortization). This figure, obtained from your financial statements, is an indicator of your operational performance and is of utmost importance to your potential selling price.*

In summary, it almost goes without saying that fixing cars, implementing processes and dealing with people is all a means to the end of making money. Never forget to learn the metrics, understand current benchmarks, and keep up with industry trends and tools to improve results and/or strategy. Then go execute to drive improved results.

CHAPTER 3 TAKEAWAYS

* Build a "franchise-like" business model that is repeatable and sustainable.
* Utilize your product suppliers' written SOPs for repairing vehicles.
* Create a standards "playbook" that encompasses the entire administrative process.
* Independently-owned repair shops can use their smaller size as an advantage for continuous improvement.
* Standards help with accountability and workplace enjoyment.
* Hold regular process improvement meetings and reinforce the standards.
* Test and audit—inspect what you expect!

* Regularly provide feedback to the team with their progress towards goals and adherence to standards.
* Measure critical process steps as much or more than you measure outcomes like CSI.
* Know your numbers. Learn to prepare, understand, and operate your business using accurate financial data.

Chapter 4

● ● ●

SECRET FOUR – GETTING CUSTOMERS TO YOUR DOOR

"Customer satisfaction is worthless.
Customer loyalty is priceless."

– JEFFREY GITOMER

Because I love this industry and the people in it, I am here to tell you the truth—and maybe not what some of you want to hear—on two controversial topics. First, if you are building a business entirely dependent on insurance direct repair programs (DRPs), I believe you are making a huge mistake. Second, much of the money many of you spend on advertising is wasted. Entire companies have been built upon taking advantage of our industry's ignorance on how to best get customers to the door. Many so-called industry experts also want you to believe that you need DRPs to succeed. While I don't inherently have anything against DRPs, I will explain why you should never build a business entirely around them. I am not sharing some flimsy opinion here with you; I base the information on real facts and experiences discovered in the real world of collision repair and what I have discovered through the science of consumer buying behaviors.

MARKETING SOLUTIONS

I am not trying to sound like a conspiracy theorist here because I believe some of these companies offering advertising, search engine optimization (SEO), and other marketing services have the right intentions, but I also know that many of them don't understand how effective marketing in our business really works. For these businesses to exist, they need you to buy into their questionable information and often will provide convincing data to support their sales pitch. The data, while impressive, often does not tell the whole truth. I promise you I have never met a collision shop owner who has built his or her fortune on Facebook likes, yet many so-called marketing companies suggest that social media should be your primary source of attracting new customers. Because most of us in the collision repair industry have never formally studied marketing or consumer buying behaviors, we honestly don't know any better than to listen to everybody's opinion about marketing. All we know is that thirty years ago, we were told by industry experts that we needed to spend anywhere from one to four percent of sales for our marketing budget. That percentage is not the problem; how we spend it is.

I do think that websites are important. I also agree that SEO and review sites such as Yelp are somewhat important, and advertising can be beneficial if done well. However, none of these things will be effective in isolation without a stout marketing plan. There is a lot to know about effective marketing and that is why people go to college to learn the craft. We need to embrace the fact that maybe as an industry we don't know as much about marketing and buying behaviors as we think we do, and we need to seek out an expert who does. That raises another problem—everybody and their brother seem to be in the body shop marketing business, and many of these firms are a waste of money unless you or they first understand "branding."

The other fact you need to know is that we are in what is known in marketing circles as an "on-demand" type of business. People don't inherently want what we have to sell. They usually hate it! Unfortunately, most people in our industry use the same forms of advertising typically appropriate for "impulse" products. Marketing on-demand products such as collision repair is relationship-driven and should be built on trust. People buy collision repair because they have to, not because they want to. This changes almost everything regarding how we should market our businesses. If you are selling restoration work or complete paint jobs, that requires a different type of plan than marketing collision repair work. That's why it is important to understand the differences before spending money on advertising.

"We have a lifetime guarantee and only perform the highest quality repairs, and we have excellent customer service." Does this pitch sound familiar? It most likely does because this information is what we as an industry typically try to sell through our advertising efforts. There are a couple of problems with this pitch. First, it is the same line everybody else uses, and second, nobody cares! If you are lucky enough to reach a person with your ad that coincidentally has just been in an accident and is shopping for collision repair services, you may stand a chance of connecting with that customer. This is assuming that you can reach him or her emotionally through your marketing efforts. Guarantees, quality repairs, and customer service are table stakes—claims every shop will make. What can you say that will connect emotionally and earn trust? This is where understanding branding comes into play. This is also the reason understanding your company's "why" is important.

WHY ARE YOU IN BUSINESS?

As the popular leadership author Simon Sinek says, "People don't buy what you do, they buy why you do it!" A great example of a company that understands this is Apple. Steve Jobs never considered his company a computer company or an iPod or iPhone company. The Apple mission statement at one point was, "To make a contribution to the world by making tools for the mind that advance humankind." Now *that* vision is powerful and how they actually live each day as a company. As a collision repair business, what is your purpose? What is your "why?" I hope you don't say to fix cars in exchange for money! When you truly understand your purpose as a company, you can then communicate it authentically to your customers and equally important, to your employees.

Your why can also become your unique value proposition that will separate you from all the other body shops. What if, through your marketing efforts, you could convey that you exist and can be trusted to help make your customers' lives better? (Notice I didn't say cars.) What if they can trust you to safely put their sons and daughters in the finished product with peace of mind? That may or may not be your unique why, but you can see how this approach would help you and your customers connect emotionally during their buying decisions. If you insist on advertising, please take the time to understand your business's "why," learn how to brand your business, understand its unique personality, as well as what it is saying to your community.

THE GREATEST SALES FORCE

Here is some great news: you already have the finest sales force in the world at your fingertips—your customers! That's right, you've heard it before and I will say it again. The best form of advertising has always been and always will be, word of mouth! I think this opportunity has been largely squandered by our industry. Again, I am not trying to sound like there is some conspiracy going on here, but there are indeed many forces out there that benefit from duping my collision repair friends into believing that their survival depends on some advertising solution or DRP program. Don't buy into it!

Marketers will try to show you research explaining why their solution is the best. They will say things like, "Here is a study showing that people make most of their buying decisions using a Smartphone," or "Here is a survey that clearly shows that insurance companies are steering sixty percent of the business to the DRP shops." While some of these facts make sense on the surface, often they don't tell the whole story. There *is* a company I do trust because they take the time to measure "the truth" properly. The company is called Phoenix Solutions Group (PSG) and they dig deep to discover what works the best to attract and keep customers for life. They are a great "marketing company" but only because they are a great "research company" first.

The real truth, and what America's greatest body shops have discovered is that when your company properly displays Confidence, Integrity, Pride and Passion to customers during the collision repair process, you will earn a customer for life who will tell friends and family about you. The problem with many of us is that we undervalue our customers. According to research done by PSG, the lifetime average sales potential of a customer is $122,000! This includes the sales derived from that customer, but more so the value derived from the referrals the customer generates through word of mouth (see research at PSG). The secret to exploiting this potential is through after-the-sale contact. Let me ask you this, if you had known that each customer had a lifetime potential value of $122,000, would you have treated him or her better? Would you have figured out how to stay in contact with that customer after the initial sale was over? I bet you would!

This is great news and an amazing opportunity for shops, but traditionally we do a poor job as an industry when it comes to retaining customers for life. We must get better to reach our potential. Another PSG study indicates that less than one in ten customers surveyed, (only 1.49 percent)[†] can even remember the name of the independent body shop that repaired their car after

---

[†] *From the Phoenix Solutions Group white paper entitled, "Collision Marketing Declassified."*

just twelve months. The results of this survey were so startling, I didn't believe it at first. I tested it out myself and found that less than one out of ten people I spoke to could remember the name of the shop that fixed their car. I would usually hear answers like, "It was that place down on Main Street across from the McDonalds." The dealership shops had a clear advantage here over the independent collision repairers when it came to name recognition. The few who did remember the shop's name often had a negative experience that connected emotionally for them, thereby locking it into their memory banks. When you combine this information with another fact, that a majority of people surveyed, (87.23 percent)‡ know a friend or family member who were in an accident, you can begin to see a serious disconnect. If this disconnect was addressed, it could represent a huge opportunity for shops because once they remember you, they can refer you!

Independent Research Results 2014:

To support the hypothesis of shops not understanding their own customer base, we draw your attention to a bank of research compiled by an independent research firm (commissioned by several paint distributors). Individuals sat in a room and answered forty-five questions regarding collision repair. All customers had their car repaired twelve months ago.

One question that stood out the most was: Name the collision repair facility that repaired your car? The percentage of customers who COULD answer: ONLY 1.49 percent.

‡ Additional research was conducted to determine a "factual" baseline of referral potential available to every shop. The scope of this research was trying to determine how many customers actually knew of someone in their circle of friends who would require the services of a collision repair facility. Over 4,000 customers were contacted who had a repair completed in the last 18 months, spanning over 135 different markets. The question that was asked of a past repair customer was: Do you know anyone else who needs the services of a collision repair facility? The percentage who answered this question with a yes—87.23 percent.

There is a huge opportunity for collision repair shops to massively increase business revenues by creating a positive and memorable experience for all customers, and then staying in contact with them during the months and years that follow. The beautiful thing is that it doesn't cost much money to begin investing in a strategy like this. Shops can clearly develop their own system for keeping in touch with customers post-sale, but I have found that most shops don't or won't invest the time necessary to do it. If this is you, there are companies that will provide this service for you. See www.bodyshopsecrets.com/resources for more information.

I have spent time with several companies that offer services designed to keep your company's name in front of customers after the sale. While I see benefits with this, you should be aware of the fundamental differences among the offerings. Some providers of these services prefer to use email as a primary source of connecting with body shop customers while others strongly believe that the U.S. Postal Service is the best way to stay in touch. I will leave it up to you to determine which delivery method is best. Personally, I appreciate receiving a personalized letter in the mail more than getting another email, but I can't tell you if everyone else feels the same. I can tell you this: Email is convenient and cheap, but it is quickly losing its effectiveness in our world of information overload.

When email was first introduced, I remember how amazing it was as a communication tool. I think most of us waited with great anticipation to get our next email message from someone we cared about. It changed the world and how we communicate, but by the new millennia, it was already becoming an easy and inexpensive way for marketers to advertise. Just like the marketers of the '80s and '90s who spent big money on mailing lists, the marketers now will go to great lengths to add you to their email lists. The Internet has become far more crowded with people trying to sell you products and services than I ever could have anticipated, and it is causing both information and email overload. It seems like I spend as much time unsubscribing from email lists than I do reading relevant emails. To be honest, most emails get deleted without ever having been read.

I am not suggesting that you cease using email or that you never use it for marketing. I am merely trying to draw your attention to its ineffectiveness as a complete tool for creating loyal customers for life, compared to more personal forms of interaction. With the overflow of information and technology we are constantly bombarded with, I believe that many of us have lost touch with humanity. As my friend, Tom Tracy from Tracy's Collision Centers says, "We have got to quit *processing* our customers!" If you want to differentiate your business, you will need to embrace what is quickly being lost— human interaction.

Another difference I notice among some of the marketing companies offering post-repair contact services is what the content of their message is. Some of these companies recommend sending out special offers or coupons. Others are proponents of sending out newsletters with helpful car-care tips. Again, this could be helpful, but what is the real message you are trying to convey? You must ask yourself, "Am I trying to manipulate the customer to come in and get a discounted wax job or am I trying to reinforce my company's commitment to Confidence, Integrity, Pride, and Passion?" These are the four areas that will get your customers to tell their friends and family about you. Do you have the guts to remind your customers through personal contact that they have a lifetime warranty and you are serious about taking care of any problems they might have with the repairs? This shows you care!

Information providers and technology companies will continue to offer newer and better "silver bullet" solutions that will allow collision repairers to easily stay in touch with customers both during and after the repair process. I believe these companies will be successful selling their tools primarily because many of us in the industry aren't willing to put in the work to create a truly exceptional customer experience. Therefore, we look to technology for help. Unfortunately, many will continue to "process" customers, believing that technology alone will satisfy customers with automated updates, texts and emails.

Consider for a moment what the experience is like when you try to call your credit card or cable company looking for assistance? How does this technological experience make you feel? How many times have you recommended your credit card or cable company to friends and family? If you do choose technology, just don't lose sight of what the customer really wants and make sure to supplement your technology with real human interaction. Many of America's greatest body shops do use technology, but none of them use technology as a replacement for a warm and memorable human experience for their customers.

THE PROBLEM WITH CSI

While I totally support measuring customer satisfaction index (CSI) scores, mainly because I like the feedback, I ask that you be aware of something. Like many things that you measure, use caution, because it doesn't always tell the whole story. We have been told for years that repeat business and referrals directly correlate to CSI scores. This is not entirely true. A shop can be lulled into a false sense of security due to a high score. I have seen several failing businesses that consistently maintained a CSI score above ninety-five percent. Even the highly-proclaimed solution called Net Promoter Score (NPS) still doesn't tell the whole story and won't guarantee that customers taking the survey will actually refer you! There is behavioral science that indicates that people must have certain emotional criteria met throughout the repair experience for them to refer you. I believe that often the customer may not even be fully conscious of these emotional triggers. The CSI questions we ask them to answer typically don't include all of the relevant questions to truly determine if they would or would not refer us. The question "On a scale of 1-10, how likely would you refer us to friends and family?" asks the customer to answer a vague question that on the surface seems to answer the most important question—but does it? What CSI or NPS doesn't measure is if the important emotional triggers that truly determine whether or not they will refer your shop have been activated.

According to behavioral science, what are the determining factors for turning customers into raving fans? The folks at Phoenix Solutions Group explain it using what they call the "Customer Experience Funnel."

CUSTOMER EXPERIENCE FUNNEL
COURTESY OF PHOENIX SOLUTIONS GROUP

Excerpt from Phoenix Solutions Group White Paper "Collision Marketing Declassified" http://www.phoenixsolutionsgroup.net/resources.html

The top portion of the funnel is titled "CONFIDENCE." This represents the beginning stage of a customer's relationship with a shop. It is measured by the courtesy of a shop's staff and whether a customer is provided a delivery date at time of drop off. These two factors are critical from the customer's perspective and begin to establish a measurable foundation of customer trust.

Traveling down the funnel to "INTEGRITY," this measurement sums up the shop's ability to "do what they say." It is measured by meeting the delivery date, the workmanship of the repair and how well the customer was communicated with during the repair. If the customer has a high degree of confidence, this area of the funnel begins to shape the strength of referral opportunities.

The third section of the funnel, titled "PRIDE," measures the shop's ability to exhibit enthusiasm for the final repair product. It is measured by the review of the warranty, how well the finished repair was reviewed and the vehicle cleaned. This section is truly a game changer in developing organic sales growth.

The last section titled, "PASSION," is the result of the three previous measurements. This indicates the percentage of customers who are passionate about the shop and measures TRUE organic growth opportunities. Measuring fully-engaged customers is a far more accurate assessment of referral opportunities than the industry-accepted metric of "would the customer refer the facility" or a net promoter score.

DIRECT REPAIR PROGRAMS

Like I mentioned earlier, I don't inherently have anything against insurance companies or direct repair programs. At one point or another throughout my career, I have probably participated in nearly every DRP program and I have many friends who work for insurance companies. They are not the devil; they are a significant part of the collision repair industry whether you like it or not. Over the last thirty plus years that I have been involved in this industry, not much has changed regarding the polarized opinions of collision repairers. Some base their entire business model around their insurance relationships, while others refuse to participate in any DRP programs, both sides stating valid opinions for the stance they take. My clients include both sides, and I respect both. I do have one strong opinion on the subject that would be a universal business principal for me regardless of which service industry I am working with. I want to have as much control over my business as possible, especially when it comes to the employee and customer experience.

A strong business is always one that understands its purpose and has defined values. If your business vision and values can include DRPs, then go for it! If not, then don't feel obligated. It's your choice either way and I am happy for you, regardless of the direction you decide to go unless you are not in alignment with your values. Many of America's greatest body shops tend to follow a hybrid thinking where they first choose customer loyalty, and then DRP if it is the right fit. They build their businesses to allow for awesome processes that ultimately support their vision to create great employee and customer experiences. If a prospective insurance partner comes along that has a DRP program that will fit into the shop's existing business model and vision without damaging the employee and customer experience, that can be a good partnership. I have participated in DRP programs that, in my opinion, added value to the employee and customer experience and unfortunately, I have participated in lousy DRPs that added no value in the long term.

This book is not intended to debate the morality of participating in DRPs, using aftermarket parts, or other political topics. I enjoy helping shops whose owners possess a variety of opinions. The one guiding value that I do stand firm on is this: Stay true to your personal and company values, and don't join a DRP program for short-term profits only to tear apart the foundational value system of your operation. If you do choose DRPs as a good fit, do not, I repeat, do not build your business growth on DRP business alone! You must have strong organic growth through customer loyalty in order to build a successful and truly sustainable business. I don't hate insurance companies, but I would never allow them to hold power over me and determine my ultimate success or failure for me!

You will find shop leaders who will fiercely debate my opinion of building a business around their DRP relationships. I'm okay with that. In fact, there are several business leaders I respect greatly for their business acumen who have chosen the path of putting DRPs on the leading edge of their growth. I found that some even ask their insurance partners where they would like them to build their next repair location. For certain shop owners, this model seems to work well. Most independent shops that have made this strategy work tend to be those that have been in business a long time and have built a significant presence in their markets long before the recent consolidation trend began. Use caution when trying to emulate these guys because this approach won't work for most of you these days. While I do respect some of these DRP-reliant shops, I still can't help wonder if they could have had equal success without all the direct repair programs.

You have a choice of the sandbox in which you want to play. As an independent collision repairer, do you want to go head-to-head with the ABRAs and Service Kings of the world competing for DRP business? Can you afford to battle with a national organization that is instantly put on every DRP program the minute it hangs a shingle? How well are your advertising solutions working against these giants? I suggest you play in the sandbox of America's greatest body shops and put customer loyalty and word-of-mouth marketing first.

When you understand some of the science behind customer loyalty and then take action, it may take a little time to get the momentum going, but before long, you will have positioned yourself with a significant advantage. Your efforts will enable you to build the sustainable business of your dreams.

OEM CERTIFICATIONS

We are already starting to see a trend where collision repair consumers are changing buying behaviors. People are increasing the number of informational sources they consult prior to making a final buying decision. These sources may include reviews on Google and Yelp, asking a friend, and so on. Guess what is trending down? Yep, DRP referrals. Word of mouth is still the king, but something else you might want to keep an eye on in the future is OEM certification programs. After listening to executives from several car makers, it has become apparent that the auto manufacturers have become cognizant of a very critical piece of information that could have a major impact on how potential accident victims are steered to a body shop. As it turns out, the manufacturers started measuring "the right things," and have discovered that brand loyalty is seriously diminished when one of their vehicles has been improperly repaired at a collision repair shop. Approximately sixty percent of vehicle owners will switch vehicle brands after a collision when the repairs were done incorrectly, according to several manufacturer representatives.

Many believe that OEMs will do whatever it takes to protect their brand by wrestling back control of how the customer gets steered, and make sure the vehicle owner ends up in a shop that can competently work on their vehicles, instead of where the insurance company wants them to go. General Motors already has the technology in place through their OnStar systems, and I know of no reason for it to stop there. Technology can instantly recognize an accident occurrence and provide the occupants with assistance that ranges anywhere from calling an ambulance to delivering the damaged vehicle to the nearest certified or approved OEM repair center. All of this takes place long before the insurance company has been notified. Having said this, there is no doubt we will also see the insurance industry fighting back with technology of their own!

Many of you reading this may be thinking, "Well that's just great for the dealership shops, but how is this technology going to help independents?" I am glad you asked. Throughout my travels around this great country, I visit a lot of dealership collision repair shops. I see some of America's greatest body shops that are dealership shops, but I also see some of the most poorly equipped and unprofessional shops that are dealer shops too! (Sorry if I offend anyone here.) I believe that the OEMs know deep down that in order to protect their precious brands, they are going to have to rely on collision repairers both inside and outside of their dealership networks. As a dealership shop in this day and age, you have a huge opportunity right now to take advantage of this trend. As an independent non-dealer collision repairer, whether a single location or regional MSO, you also have a great opportunity to capitalize on the benefits available with manufacturer certification programs because they need you too! Several OEMs have admitted they have come to the realization that they will also need to look outside of their dealership networks to find enough qualified collision repair centers.

A few shops that are already on OEM certification programs are not reporting a favorable return on investment. There are several reasons this may be true, and some self-imposed by not taking advantage of the marketing opportunities available. Even if you are not currently experiencing a big return, or are reluctant to join a certification program because you are not convinced of the potential return on investment (ROI), my advice is that you keep an open mind. I believe these programs will begin paying off big time as the OEMs are figuring out how to steer customers to you. Next, I ask you to consider that many of the equipment and training requirements for joining certification programs are needed regardless to repair the vehicles of today properly.

COMMUNITY INVOLVEMENT

I cannot complete a chapter on getting customers to your door without mentioning the importance of community involvement. Nearly all of America's greatest body shops have created a brand identity in their community whether or not they realize it. Community involvement comes in many forms but usually involves, well, involvement. I don't believe it is enough to simply advertise at the local baseball field or have an ad in the local high school paper, although I think that is okay, as long as you don't expect a big return on your investment. The shops I have seen that really benefit are committed to making a positive difference in their communities. They don't approach their involvement with a taker's attitude, but instead a giver's attitude.

Recently, I was very impressed with a campaign being done at several 1Collision Network shops that donated a vehicle to the local fire department to perform extraction exercises at their shops. This created a lot of good press and a feeling of goodwill in those communities.

I also love what Tracy's Collision Centers in Lincoln, Nebraska do each year just before Christmas. They rebuild a car and give it to someone in need in their local area. This creates a huge buzz, but more importantly, gives back to the community. Shop employees and other members of the community get involved with a great deal of pride and passion—a huge win on several levels.

> *"I guess as it is in life, those businesses that give unselfishly, seem to be rewarded, while those that only want to take, don't."*

As a second-generation body shop owner, Tom Tracy of Tracy's Collision Centers said he always dreamed of being a businessman. Since taking over the family body shop in Lincoln, Nebraska during the 1980s, the business has grown to include two shops and fifty employees. Tracy has found multiple benefits over the years from implementing marketing initiatives and building a brand, as well connecting with the community and others in the industry.

Tom Tracy, Tracy's Collision Centers

CASE STUDY: TOM TRACY – TRACY'S COLLISION CENTERS

Our customer focus for the most part is: be friendly, be kind, be good. We try to make sure that our customers are going to come back. A few years ago, we were introduced to Steve Schoolcraft from Phoenix Solutions Group at an AkzoNobel conference. I gave it a lot of thought, and we started a relationship with him.

Our takeaways from the partnership really helped how we delivered cars and engaged customers. He would come twice a year to Lincoln and have dinner with our office personnel to talk about our results. We were already doing well, and I think we started to do a better job. It's one of many things that ended up helping us in our marketplace.

I think what makes us unique is we work very hard to market our business. I've been mainly engaged in marketing for the company since I started working as the CEO and had a lot of good mentors, whether they were from radio or television.

I went to several marketing events that were put on by either the television or radio industries. During one of the most effective events I attended, they said you have to advertise like Coca-Cola. The whole nature of that statement is to break it down and say, "If I follow these basic advertising theories, something good is going to happen." I agreed with that and we established a different campaign.

Then we came up with a slogan, "Thanks Lincoln." Part of that came from an idea that hatched from Steve Schoolcraft about how you should be thanking your customers. It became a huge success.

It brought to life repeat customers and all of the goodwill we had going for us. It was just phenomenal what came from that. We've been busy pretty much for as long as I can remember.

I think one thing a lot of shops haven't focused on enough in the past is marketing and building a brand. When you have to write a check to build a brand, sometimes it's not that easy to do, but you have to pound the drum. Sometimes major media, whether it be television or radio, is the only way you can get enough attention to build that brand. You need to figure out how to do that efficiently and you have to stay engaged in it long enough to make it work for you. Once you do that, you have a lot of marketing power.

It's like a snowball rolling down a hill. Once you get it big enough, and you've been doing it long enough, your brand is established.

I think it's important to drive people to your website too. We've done more of that in the last couple of years. It's where people can learn more about what you are doing. It makes a difference. People might spend five or six minutes on your site and then they will have an idea about what they are getting.

When marketing a body shop, what you're really selling is trust, and that's what people really care about.

Through the AkzoNobel 20 group we were involved with, we challenged each other to donate a car. This was before Recycled Rides started, which we were part of later. This last December, we gave away our twenty-first and twenty-second cars at an event.

Five years ago, we started a relationship with the Lincoln Children's Museum and built what we refer to as our third location. In an area of the museum called Tiny Town, they have Tracy's Collision Centers where kids can practice tuning up a car and applying paint.

We made some television commercials to support the museum and bring awareness to the exhibit. I had two *different customers tell me that they came to the shop because they took their grandkids to the Children's Museum and they were so impressed we would support the museum with an exhibit they decided this is where they wanted to get their car fixed.*

We also became involved in a community action group called Lincoln Lancaster Community Action. They manage Head Start and a lot of other government programs. That has been a great relationship. We started a Head Start classroom with our name on it last year, which has been kind of fun.

Community involvement does a lot of good for your employees because it offers them a chance to give of themselves and their talents. We've done it for a long time so it's something they look forward to. Our goal with the car giveaway is to change somebody's life and I think we've been able to do that.

CHAPTER 4 TAKEAWAYS

* Take time to learn branding before spending more money on advertising.
* Identify your company's purpose or "why."
* Beware of the marketing solutions available and choose the right expert.
* Word-of-mouth marketing has always been and always will be the best form of advertising.
* If you use technology to stay in touch with your customers, supplement it with human touch.

* Don't get lulled into a false sense of security through CSI scores.
* Learn how to display Confidence, Integrity, Pride and Passion into each customer experience.
* Be part of a DRP if it fits your business model, but never build your business entirely around DRPs.
* Get involved in your community!

Chapter 5

• • •

SECRET FIVE – MODERN LEADERSHIP

*"You can do what I cannot do. I can do what you
cannot do. Together we can do great things."*

– Mother Teresa

Understanding the difference between a manager and a leader
is a good place to start as you begin the transformation into
a successful modern-day collision repair business. We hire
managers to run our companies based on their organizational
skills, vehicle knowledge, and how well they get things done.
We hope that they are able to influence people to work hard
and help the company make more money through their efforts.
The problem is that many managers don't know much about
being a leader. Leadership has little to do with being the boss; it
is more than a title. Leadership is a privilege reserved for those
who wish to serve, not be served. Modern leadership is often
referred to as "servant leadership" because it is one of the leader's

responsibilities to ensure that the team has everything needed to be successful. Successful leaders understand that people will follow you if you lead because it is impossible to lead when you are only pushing your people from behind.

> *"Leadership is a privilege reserved for those who wish to serve, not be served."*

Does your staff view each new attempt at process change as just another "flavor of the month" that is rarely embraced? Why?

Here are two "whys:"

* Why are you in business?
* Why should the staff care?

WHY ARE YOU IN BUSINESS?

This simple question stumps many. Why do you do what you do? Is the reason you get out of bed every day just to ensure the bills are paid or do you have a more noble reason for running a collision repair business? The sad fact is that many shop owners forget why they started their businesses to begin with—their dreams now gone with the distant past. The harsh realities of the daily grind have changed the original *why* of great joy and passion to what is now mere survival.

What does this have to do with getting people to do what you want and creating lasting change? It has <u>everything</u> to do with it! Values and vision are at the very foundation of every great organization. If you don't know the *why,* how are you going to have a guiding vision in the first place?

First, you must deeply think about your *why.* Think about the dreams you had when you first began operating a body shop. Find that passionate person inside and bring him or her back! What does your business model look and feel like in your dreams? In your dreams, is your shop the one techs would love to come to work for and all your customers are raving fans? Are you enjoying your time at work?

Once you have documented your *why,* it is time to shout it out to the world! It becomes the culture of your business and then you can begin to share the vision with your employees.

WHY SHOULD THE STAFF CARE?

Industrial-age thinking views employee satisfaction and motivation primarily as a product of money. In Daniel Pink's book, *DRIVE,* he states: "The best use of money as a motivator is to pay people enough to take the issue of money off the table." Pink then goes on to say, "But once we've cleared the table, carrots and sticks can achieve precisely the opposite of their intended aims."

In other words, paying people what they are worth is critical to fulfill their basic needs, but beyond that, throwing money at employee problems usually doesn't work. I believe that many of us still use this technique because we don't understand modern leadership skills.

THREE FUNDAMENTAL LEADERSHIP STEPS

There are three fundamental leadership steps to encourage people to follow you and your change initiatives. Obviously, there is a lot more to leadership and influence skills than this, but if you can get these three right, you are well on your way!

1. **Learn how to communicate with people**

    In order to encourage people to openly communicate with you, you need to re-learn how to communicate. Modern leadership involves creating a safe environment for people to speak freely with one another. Time spent just listening to your staff with your ego removed is critical to the development of a healthy culture. Communication skills are paramount to all other leadership skills in my opinion, and by simply making it safe for people to open up to you, it will make a huge difference over time.

2. **Tie intrinsic values to key behaviors**

    If you want your staff on board with change initiatives, you must learn to tie your employees' intrinsic values to key behaviors. Intrinsic value is another way of saying "what your employees are passionate about."

    These crucial conversations will allow you to successfully explain why change is important to both the company's success and the individuals involved. To illustrate this, imagine speaking to your body tech about the importance of thorough disassembly as being critical to the success of blueprinting. This tech commonly complains about all of the delays poorly written estimates cause him. The problem does have a financial impact, but what upsets him the most is that every time he gets started on a vehicle, he runs into another supplement. Too many leaders might write him off as a chronic complainer and not act any further. He values continuous production and it is your job as a modern-day leader to connect the dots for him as to why the thorough disassembly will help eliminate his pain. You have then connected his intrinsic values (continuous production) to key behaviors (thorough disassembly).

3. **Share the vision**
   By following the previous steps, you will have built a foundation of trust and respect. This foundation allows you to successfully share your *why* with the team. Your *why*, when connected to the intrinsic values of your people, becomes a powerful culture. You must passionately paint this vision every day while being cautious of acting contrary to it. Every time you turn a blind eye on your *why* or your vision, you quickly lose respect, and your integrity suffers.

   Having created a culture where everyone understands the vision, change initiatives such as those used in lean methods become much easier to execute. If, for example, you want to implement a new blueprinting program, you gather your people and explain why blueprinting is important to the company's vision. You connect the behaviors necessary for successful blueprinting (such as thorough disassembly) to their intrinsic values (continuous production, or whatever it might be) and then you ask for their input on the best way to implement blueprinting at your shop (buy-in).

TECHNICIAN SHORTAGES AND MILLENNIALS

Everyone in our industry seems to be complaining about technician shortages and they are also complaining about the work ethic of the millennial generation. These concerns are understandable, but when you are viewing this situation from outside your victim zone, you may realize that a sizable portion of our employee shortages are actually our fault as business leaders.

I agree that there is an aging workforce in our industry, and a reluctant new workforce entering our trade, as well as most other trades. I have a lot of theories about why this is, but let's focus on what you can do about it. After all, we want to be proactive, right? Let's start with the technician shortage and bust some bad thinking about this subject. A decade or so ago, technicians would jump ship for a dollar more an hour offered by the competitor down the street. Chances are, in the old days, he or she had already worked for the competitor down the street once before, and chances are also good that he or she would probably be working for you again as the revolving door of technicians continued. Today, things are a little different in the sense that employees are offered slightly better working conditions and benefits. Bigger companies offer great benefits, which is helping to keep techs in place longer, so the revolving door is starting to slow down. With a smaller number of new people entering the workforce, and employees not wanting to jump ship so quickly, we find ourselves in trouble when we do have someone leave our employ. The exception to this is when consolidation hits your town. For the first couple years, you will notice a lot of people movement until things settle down, and then it becomes hard to find new hires again.

Knowing that it is challenging to attract new workers, America's greatest body shops don't wait until they desperately need someone and then hire the first potentially incompetent person that comes along. The best shops work on recruitment proactively. In other words, they interview and reach out to potential employees even when they don't have a spot on the roster for them yet. They begin the process of building relationships with potential future employees that will fit their business model and their culture. For growing companies, this is a must! I am sure you know how dysfunctional the cultures can be at shops that always hire out of desperation, so don't let this happen to you!

I also like what I am seeing at some of the larger organizations like the MSO consolidators, Service King and ABRA Auto Body and Glass. They are working with local schools in an organized recruitment and development process that will increase the likelihood that they will have a steady supply of technicians who are trained the right way. If you are thinking that your company is too small to engage in such activities, I invite you to challenge your beliefs! As a smaller independently-owned company, there are still many ways that you can get involved with local schools to create a program that will allow you to keep tabs on good talent and ensure they are trained the right way as they move up through the ranks at your shop. One of the keys is to develop your own defined career path that you can use to help young people understand the steps necessary to reach their goals and yours.

I hate to generalize any generation, but what is known about the millennial generation is that they value "meaning in life" more than other generations. I would never say that they are not motivated by money, but for many young people, money does not take precedence when considering a career. Money to them is a tool that allows the freedom to explore other passions in life. Remember the paragraph urging you to consider your "why?" If you want millennials to come to work for you, and better yet, stay for a while, you need to lead with your "why." These youngsters are smart enough to want to contribute to something more meaningful than just wrenching on a car in exchange for a buck. Make sure they know WHY wrenching on that car makes a difference in someone's life, and how their efforts are contributing to the mission of the company.

In 2010, while working for Bradshaw Collision Centers, we began experimenting with how we administratively staffed our locations. We had known for some time that certain estimators excelled at people skills while others felt more comfortable hanging out in the shops with the technicians. During this time, we also questioned whether some of the people we had in leadership positions were really qualified to lead in the first place. We discovered that far too many people, even though they had strong skills in certain areas, were actually sitting in the wrong seats. We also found it daunting and time-consuming to keep shuffling employees around until we finally found a combination that worked. We felt there had to be a better way to figure this mess out. That is when I was introduced to Kevin Wolfe and his company, LeadersWay.

Upon meeting Kevin and his LeadersWay team, I quickly became immersed in and fascinated with behavioral science. The process began with the LeadersWay team having me complete an online assessment they refer to as the "Trimetrix Assessment" that would give them insight on what my personality was like, my skills, what motivates me, and even how I feel about my life. The next day, after completing this assessment, Kevin contacted me to discuss the results of the assessment. I was shocked! The results were incredibly revealing and even drew attention to some of my less-than-perfect traits (yes, I have them too). It is also important to note that the real value of the assessment was not to point out what a jerk I could be, but instead to create awareness about how I could be coming across to other people without realizing it. The debriefing process also included recommended coaching strategies for someone with my personality profile. Learning the truth about oneself may be scary, but it is only after discovering it that people can begin to improve themselves, their lives, and the lives of those around them.

COACHING

Besides the Trimetrix Assessment being transformational to me personally, it also proved to be hugely transformational back at Bradshaw's. We required all administrative staff in leadership or sales positions to take the assessment, and the outcome was even more eye-opening. It became very clear that not only did we have a lot of people in the wrong positions, but we had people that didn't even want to be working at Bradshaw's at all! With the help of the LeadersWay team, we began working to build a better team. We coached some people, became better at listening to employees' needs, helped a couple find jobs elsewhere, and began positioning people in jobs where they would excel. The assessment also proved to be a reliable tool we could use with new hires, cutting out months from the usual learning curve typically required when getting to know someone and their work habits.

Since those days, I now use these assessments with many of the clients I coach and mentor and several of my clients also utilize them so they can run smarter businesses. In our industry, we talk a lot about having difficulty attracting new workers; not enough of the talk is about what it takes to build and retain a good team. Employee satisfaction is at the very foundation of every great company. I believe that companies that ignore this advice will not succeed at having great customer service or sustainable customer loyalty, since having happy customers is a result of having happy employees. It is time to take advantage of the science that is available to help your business and take some of the guesswork out of the recruitment process.

Thanks to my experience with Kevin Wolfe and his LeadersWay team, I was not only introduced to the value of the Trimetrix Assessment, but also something I found to be even more beneficial in terms of the development of people and companies: coaching. I credit coaching not only for my own personal development over the years since meeting Kevin, but also the primary reason my company has been successful helping others. The fundamental difference between Elite and the competition is our approach to helping clients reach their potential. In other words, my company doesn't just provide advice, we are trained to bring the best out of our clients, to make the best out of the knowledge they already possess. I am sharing this information with you because coaching is a skill that anyone can learn if they put their mind to it, and any individual or organization can reap amazing benefits.

When folks think of coaching, they usually envision a sports coach. Images of great coaches, like Vince Lombardi or Bear Bryant, giving a fiery halftime speech come to mind. While I love these guys and study many great coaches and sports figures, this is not exactly what I am referring to. Success coaching only rarely, if ever, involves giving an inspiring speech. Instead, the coach asks a lot of questions that help coachees discover obstacles in their lives and the thinking that could be holding them back from reaching their full potential. It is very common for people in a variety of occupations who wish to reach the top of their fields to turn to professional coaching. So why don't people in the collision repair business hire coaches? That is a fair question, and I can tell you that most people in our industry don't, and I can also tell you that only a very small handful of people in collision repair come anywhere close to reaching their full potential when they have every opportunity to do so!

> *"Only a very small handful of people in collision repair come anywhere close to reaching their full potential when they have every opportunity to do so!"*

Another great opportunity is to learn the skill of coaching yourself. Since coaching is a skill that involves asking questions and doing more listening than talking, I highly recommend everyone in a leadership position learn this valuable skill. You don't necessarily need to become a certified coach, but everyone who is serious about building a great company with a great team and a great culture will need to learn some coaching skills. The best way to do this is to either reach out to a company like LeadersWay, such as I did, or learn from reading books and watching videos on coaching. Our resource page provides some great places to get started: www.bodyshopsecrets.com/resources.

I ask you to consider the power of asking questions for a moment. Asking the right questions can help people transform lives, but have you ever considered the power of asking questions in other situations? Leadership by its very definition is the ability to influence people to follow you. Influencing people to do what you want is a crucial skill and not to be confused with its sleazy distant cousin "manipulation." Influence skills are some of the most important skills one can possess in order to become truly successful in life as a leader, in the sales profession, or life in general. The greatest salespeople in the world have mastered their questions. Learning to better understand the needs of a potential customer is at the very heart of great salesmanship just as it is trying to convince an employee to follow you as a leader. Every one of us is "in sales" whether you know it or not, why not become great at it?

About ten years ago, Tony Adams recognized that the leadership style that had made his Kansas body shop successful in the past, was no longer effective in the modern world. The culture at Weaver's Auto Center was quickly deteriorating. He decided to search for a coach and began incorporating a servant-leadership philosophy and set of practices in his business. He said it was the best decision he ever made.

*From left to right: Tony Adams, Jheu Cruz and
Todd Timbrook, Weaver's Auto Center*

CASE STUDY: TONY ADAMS – WEAVER'S AUTO CENTER

*In 2008, I was going through a difficult patch in my business,
like we all go through from time to time, and a great friend of
mine, Dale Opeka, told me that I needed coaching. He recommended that I call Kevin Wolfe from LeadersWay.*

*What I thought of as coaching was Little League. I told him
that I didn't need someone cheering me on—ra ra ra. I was
hesitant to even call Kevin at first but Dale was really persis-
tent and I finally contacted him. It was one of the best decisions I ever made. Kevin helped mold me into the person I am
today and I am forever grateful for that.*

The first book he had me read is the One Minute Manager Meets the Monkey. *It's all about how we as leaders take on other people's "monkeys" and we think we are trying to help.*

I began learning and understanding the different principles and philosophies around servant leadership.

I learned about three types of leaders: "do for," "do to" and "do with." I was the "do for" type. I didn't want my employees to work late and be here on Saturdays so I would do the work for them thinking that I was helping and protecting them. In this type of situation, at some point in time you get frustrated and irritated because you are the one who is doing all the work. Then you get mad and become a "do to" manager and say, "I'm not going to do this work anymore—you do it." Afterwards, you feel bad about doing that and then you go back into that "do for" model. It's a vicious cycle.

After I finished the book, I had several people in the office read it as well. I wanted to make sure everybody understood where I was coming from and start addressing cultural development. If you take the word 'cult' out of culture without the negative connotations, at the end of the day what is a cult? It's a group of people who are connected to a common leader, a common belief system and speak a common language.

One of the first things I worked on was developing a common language. I couldn't just come in and say, "OK, I'm not doing this for you anymore." Instead, it was becoming comfortable saying, "If I have to do this for you, then I don't need you," and not coming from a place that was threatening by any means. It was understanding and sharing with employees that, "It's not my job doing it for you; that's why we hired you." It's a trap that I think a lot of managers and leaders get into.

The place we want to be is "do with." Let's do this together and make sure you understand it before we just throw you in to sink or swim. I also learned the importance of having clear, written expectations of our employees and communicating those expectations. I realized that if I don't know what to expect of my employees, how will they ever know?

In the past, I used an industrial-age management style— managing by fear— "I say jump and you ask how high?" The leadership style of the 21st century is about growing and supporting people and operating from a servant-leader mindset.

The biggest pill I had to swallow was my ego. It wasn't my people who were the problem. It was me.

One of the hardest things I think for people to understand, at least with leaders at the top of their organizations, is that it's always a leadership issue. Very rarely is it a people issue although I'm not saying that organizations don't have some employees who have some bad behaviors.

Once I became clear on that, I had a conversation with everybody—sometimes daily. I told them, 'This is the direction that we are going to go as a company and I know there are people on my team who are not going to be here as we continue to move forward. I don't know who those people are and I certainly can't imagine losing anybody on my team but I'm not going to negotiate on what I want and expect. Some people are just going choose along the way that they don't want to be part of this journey. And that's ok too.'

For the employees, I think it was a mixed emotion of happiness and frustration. Some didn't like it because there are people who take advantage and like a manager who does everything for them. The superior performers on the team loved it because they could see some of those poor performers out there and were glad that I was holding people accountable.

The first major shift was understanding that we are an employee-first organization. My employees come first. I want to make sure they are happy, healthy and fully engaged. If they are, they are going to be in a better position to take care of our customers. If our customers are happy, healthy and engaged in what we are doing in our business, then profits and revenue follow that. The way it impacted our organization is the teamwork we have now. It's not uncommon to come into our business and see three or four techs working on one car at a time. It has become a culture of collaboration and working together. They are making good, strong friendships within the organization. It's not every man for himself. Everyone is after one common goal. We're not just after the almighty dollar; we're after something bigger.

I recommend that other shops interested in making changes start reading, learning and understanding that there are different ways to lead and talk and communicate.

There are many books on the subject. Our brain is a muscle just like any other muscle in our body and it will atrophy when we stop using it.

I also recommend hiring a coach. Many shops will hire someone to market their business, to come and learn lean processes and how to revamp administration scanning and filing. Why wouldn't you hire a coach to help you with what you don't know from a leadership perspective?

We've learned a lot along the way about servant-leadership, behavioral science and having clear expectations. This has helped us create the culture we have now. The biggest thing in leadership is having the right heart and coming from the right place and understanding that you need to be there for your employees.

CHAPTER 5 TAKEAWAYS

* Learn modern leadership skills to lead instead of being a boss.
* Understand your company's "why."
* Be proactive about recruiting the right people for your organization.
* Create a meaningful culture where millennials will want to work.
* Consider using talent assessments to place the right people in the right seats.
* Hire a coach if you want to reach your potential.
* Learn coaching skills to become a better leader.
* Learn influence and sales skills.

Chapter 6

SECRET SIX – THE POWER OF PEER GROUPS

*"Surround yourself only with people
who are going to take you higher."*

— OPRAH WINFREY

I recently attended an MSO (multiple store operator) sympo-sium at an industry convention, and was disappointed by one of the statements repeatedly made during a panel discussion. "I believe you must become an MSO in the future if you are going to survive." Hogwash! It is not the first time I have heard this nonsense, and I am pretty certain you have heard it too. Look, I get it. There are, in fact, advantages of scale by being an MSO, but survival has more to do with operational excellence than the number of stores you own. I can point out many shops, some mentioned in this book, that are running a single location much better than their local MSO competitors. I see their financial data and what might surprise many is that it quite often indicates they are actually outperforming their MSO competitors overall with only a single store!

A problem I do see however, is when single location operators forget who their customer is, and compete head-to-head for insurance business with all of the consolidator shops that have settled in around them. This doesn't usually work out too well.

Don't get me wrong. I love nothing more than to see entrepreneurs grow into multiple locations, but please make sure you get the first one right before expanding. If you have too many headaches dealing with one, adding several more is probably not going to make your problems disappear. Remember secret three—you must build a sustainable business model first, and then grow. What some experts don't realize when making these definitive doom-and-gloom statements is that first, single store collision repairers who are operating properly can indeed survive, and second, many of the advantages the MSOs have can be gained by participation in a peer group.

The power of peer groups was first introduced to me in the classic book *Think and Grow Rich* by Napoleon Hill. The book is essentially a study of how the greatest men in America became great. (Kind of like this book!) Studies of extraordinary men such as Andrew Carnegie and Henry Ford revealed that the great industrialists of their time credited much of their success to their ability to surround themselves with people who knew things they did not. The "Mastermind Principle," as it was called in the book, is still a leading reason that ordinary men and women rise to greatness. A mastermind group is an organized effort of two or more people working toward a definite purpose in the spirit of harmony. You too can possess this power through deciding today to hang out with winners—by associating with people who share your passion to succeed in the collision repair business. These people can be found in several places, including associations, franchises and performance groups.

ASSOCIATIONS

Don't underestimate how crucial associations are to the collision repair industry's future prosperity, especially for the independent repair community. As a young entrepreneur in the late '80s and early '90s, my affiliation with the Oregon Auto Body Craftsman Association (OACA) was priceless. I was a very young man, and had much to learn. At the time, my shop was tiny, dirty and poorly equipped. I honestly didn't know what I was doing, although I could paint a car better than most people. I was introduced to Janet Chaney, who was the executive director of the association. She must have taken pity on me because she allowed me to join the group shortly after. The members of the OACA took me under their wing; I learned a lot and created friendships that have lasted my entire lifetime.

The group meetings often involved a lot of socializing and good times, but the group also got a lot of important work done. We became a force to be reckoned with in the Oregon State Legislature by introducing and passing laws to help the industry improve. We brought valuable education to the members and helped Oregon develop a reputation in the country for having some of the nation's best shops. The OACA truly made the industry a better place and I have to say that since then I haven't seen a local community full of tough competitors get along so well. Unfortunately, the subject of DRPs became the group's demise.

I tell you this because it is an important lesson to be learned about associations. The OACA, once one of the country's most powerful associations, was quickly brought to its knees by a handful of its members whose political views outweighed their dedication to the success of the overall group. I don't mind people having their values and opinions around politics, religion or direct repair programs, but small-minded people have a way of making their agendas more important than everyone else's, and it can do a great deal of harm, especially in an association. Key members of the group, people I looked up to, were forced off the board of directors (through a secretive proxy battle) because of their views on direct repair programs. This included my dear friend Janet Chaney, who was removed from her position as executive director. It was truly a very sad day and the beginning of the end for the Oregon Auto Body Craftsmen Association.

As was mentioned in the first chapter of this book, people coming together can be powerful, but it can also be powerfully negative—especially if you choose to associate with a group of small-minded people who continually blame their problems on everyone else. A powerful collision repair association is a group of people dedicated to helping one another be successful and overcoming the challenges that we all face together. If you feel that DRPs are bad for the industry, I respect your views, but please understand that a healthy association or peer group focuses on business excellence, regardless of whether its members are DRP shops. Sadly, this country is filled with far too many groups that meet only to reinforce each other's negativity during a good old-fashioned pity party! These are not the groups you will see America's greatest body shops attending.

The good news is that there are many good association groups around the country that shops can join to help get leaders out of their bubble and benefit greatly. Both the Automotive Service Association (ASA) and the Society of Collision Repair Specialists (SCRS) have many local groups all over the United States. These groups can provide you with a tremendous amount of shared knowledge, buying power for various products or services, and fellowship that will help keep you inspired.

In talking with SCRS Executive Director, Aaron Schulenburg, his view of associations similarly echoed the value of surrounding yourself with positive people.

I've been predisposed to association involvement for most of my career. The first repair facility I ever worked for—Dan's Paint and Body in Tucson, Arizona—was a big advocate of industry involvement, and the owner was the president of our state association. He encouraged my involvement in association activities at a national level because he wanted to give back to an industry that had done a lot for him. He also understood the value of having team members working shoulder-to-shoulder with other innovative small business owners who had both a grasp of the challenges facing the industry and an inclination to try and impact them in a positive manner.

Being an active member of an association gives you a circle of influence that can make you sharper, and helps shape the direction in which you position your business for the future. There is value in the information you receive as a more passive recipient of information as well, but the real magic happens when you get directly involved in the meetings and the efforts. I think this is often easiest at a state level, and then that opens the door to the value of national level involvement in a group like SCRS.

That grassroots level of volunteerism is exactly what built SCRS, and continues to drive its efforts today. Resources like Repairer Driven News (www.repairerdrivennews.com), the Database Enhancement Gateway (www.degweb.org) and the Guide to Complete Repair Planning (www.scrs.com) were all association initiatives that developed from people who were in the thick of industry issues brainstorming on a better way to deliver the help the industry needed, and then relying on the power of associations to accomplish it and get it to the masses.

To be honest, the optimism I see for the future of our industry is entirely shaped by looking around our table and seeing an ever-evolving group of individuals who are passionate about this industry, and even more so about leaving it better than they found it. Membership is a mechanism to take advantage of the benefits and resources of the group, but to also support the volunteerism of those folks who are working hard on your behalf. I think there are very few people you will ever talk to that will feel they paid more than they received in value from an association like SCRS.

See our website resource page for more information about how to find a good association in your area: www.bodyshopsecrets. com/resources.

WOMEN'S INDUSTRY NETWORK (WIN)

In the fall of 2015, I was asked to speak to a group of women from the collision repair industry. On the stage the following May, I was scheduled to follow the great Gold Medal gymnast and cancer survivor, Shannon Miller. No pressure, right? In front of me sat nearly two hundred of the collision repair industry's most successful women. At that moment, I felt as though things could go very right or perhaps, very wrong! Thankfully, I survived. I was so grateful to have been given this opportunity and meet so many amazing women. I feel as though the contributions made by many of these talented women from the Women's Industry Network (WIN) may go unnoticed in our male-dominated industry, but make no mistake, we have an amazing presence of women in our industry and in many different facets.

I met female shop owners, managers, women working in high-level positions in the insurance industry, vendor companies and technicians. I'm here to tell you we are in no short supply of talented leaders with WIN around! I believe that in the future we will continue to see more and more women moving into key leadership positions in repair shops. I must admit that most of the women I have met through WIN and in shops possess natural leadership skills, such as empathy and listening skills, more so than many of their male counterparts. It was both inspiring and encouraging to meet the younger WIN members as well. I feel much better about the future of our industry since having learned about the Women's Industry Network.

One of the key activities that makes WIN such a successful group is their mentorship program. Young women who are new to the industry are paired with a mentor to help guide them on their journey into the industry. I feel that mentorship is so important for anyone who wants to succeed. I highly encourage the women reading this book to become part of the Women's Industry Network. There are also plenty of opportunities for men to support this group. See our website's resource page for more information: www.bodyshopsecrets.com/resources.

Petra Schroeder, chair of the Women's Industry Network, said the non-profit organization is dedicated to encouraging, developing and cultivating opportunities to attract women to collision repair. Now retired after working in the industry and for the same company for forty-seven years, the "Collisionista" remains active in WIN.

I retired from my beloved career in July 2016 but decided to stay involved in this industry because it has been so good to me over the years. It has been a very satisfying and successful career at Axalta (formerly DuPont) and I want to give back as much as I can. I currently chair WIN, serve as secretary of the Collision Industry Foundation (CIF) and attend industry meetings and events year-round.

At the end of 2016, WIN had five hundred and eight members, including thirty men. When we were formed in 2006, nobody thought we would ever have five hundred plus members. However, our membership continues to grow. It includes people from every segment of collision repair— body shops, suppliers, technology providers, insurance companies, manufacturing and education segments— across the entire United States and Canada.

WIN is a totally volunteer-driven organization. Nobody is paid for what they do. Currently, we have nineteen directors on our board and there are a lot of volunteer opportunities to take part in. WIN is almost like a miniature company with a balance sheet, budget, strategic plans and various committees. My hope is to entice more of our WIN members to get engaged in one or more of these twelve committees and make WIN an even more beneficial part of the collision repair industry. What this does is it creates opportunities for leadership development and other skills important for success.

WIN offers scholarships and financial awards to college students for tuition assistance, educational opportunities, and enrichment events to the awardees. Such WINners are paired with a WIN board member or a Most Influential Women's (MIW) award winner who stays in contact with these young women.

Besides coaching and mentoring young women, we also constantly learn from each other. If I don't have the answer to a question or need a sounding board, there is a network of fellow WIN members out there.

As result of our strategic planning, we are in the process of revamping and reviewing our scholarship program and planning to pilot local networking groups. It is a lot of fun to be part of WIN and has enriched my life in many ways.

FRANCHISES

My second real job as a kid was as a "masker" at a Maaco franchise located in Salem, Oregon. All I did was tape up cars all day long for minimum wage. Most of the jobs were complete paint jobs for used car dealers, but we also painted some vehicles for consumers wanting to spruce up the family grocery-getter. I worked with a fellow named Lupe who taught me the fastest methods for taping up a car. He was only half my height, but he could tape up an entire Coupe de Ville in under forty-five minutes—scripted emblems and all! The color changes took a little longer because we had to mask off around the door jambs too. Lupe and his brother, who also worked there as a "sander," were both very nice to me and spent time teaching me all the systems that had made them successful doing their job. I was usually too broke to buy my lunch, so Lupe, his brother, and some of the other Hispanic guys would give me a few of the pickled jalapenos they shared during the lunch break. They watched with great delight as I struggled to eat the spicy little peppers. During these lunches, they taught me all the systems they had learned from the Maaco organization's trainers. They were all very efficient at their jobs, whether it was masking, sanding, or taking dents out. I began to learn at a very young age the importance of standard operating procedures and best practices.

Even though we were doing cheaper, lower-quality paint jobs than some shops, it was the systems that impressed me. I learned that if you had the right systems in place, you could produce any level of quality you wanted to—and do it consistently. Like Lupe and the others who I worked with, they had learned the best possible way to perform their jobs; not through many years of trial and error, but by learning it from someone else who had already perfected it. These are the proven systems that can make franchises, like Maaco, so valuable. From advertising power to group purchasing power to best practices, for many shop owners, franchising is a good option. Some franchise groups also bring along the added benefit of built-in direct repair relationships, if that is important to you and your shop.

CARSTAR has been a big name in our industry and a good partner to independent collision repairers for many years. CARSTAR Auto Body Repair Experts is North America's largest multi-shop operator network of independently-owned and operated collision repair facilities with more than five hundred locations in the U.S. and Canada. It will be interesting to watch the course of CARSTAR, since the company's purchase by Driven Brands in 2015. I believe their group president, Jose Costa, is a very experienced and well-respected franchise leader. CARSTAR franchisees that I have spoken to are also excited about the future direction. CARSTAR has relationships with several insurers, as well as DRP opportunities for its Best in Class franchisees that meet certain performance criteria.

Fix Auto USA has a strong U.S. presence with more than one hundred locations operating in eight states, and is a preeminent collision repair brand. Fix Auto's commitment to enabling independently-owned body shops with a platform so that they can compete in a consolidating and competitive marketplace can be seen in every facet of their brand—from operational support to marketing programs to a community of like-minded operators. Their mission is to only invite those who are passionate and deeply engaged with their business, driven towards continued excellence, and who are progressive, forward thinkers.

Part of a broader organization, Fix Auto is a global network of independently-owned body shops with more than four hundred twenty-five locations. Globally, Fix Auto operates in eight countries: Australia, Canada, China, France, South Africa, Turkey, U.K., and the U.S.

Fix Auto is committed to strict location consistency with both branding and process. As you would expect, this provides a great deal of efficiency and predictability that, ultimately, benefits their customers—insurance companies and vehicle owners. Lastly, Fix Auto locations have access to several national DRP relationships, and from my experience, have excellent KPI reporting capabilities, and impressive centralized call center capabilities.

1Collision Network is an impressive franchise network organization that has recently been attracting a lot of press. Originating in the Chicago and Milwaukee markets, the group has expanded into the south and west, and are targeting strategic areas throughout the U.S. 1Collision offers similar benefits to the other franchise organizations, as well as a few valuable and unique services, with a "friendly" price of entry. There are many add-on solutions offered, as needed by the shop. 1Collision does require a unique branding "makeover" but franchisees do not need to abandon their name. This company has effective marketing solutions, product and equipment buying power, and their 1Collision Performance System offers top-notch process development.

If you are interested in becoming a franchisee, I recommend that you do your homework to decide which one would be the best fit for your shop. Also, know that there are several other franchise organizations other than those I have mentioned for you to consider.

"But wait!" I can hear some of you saying now, "Dave, I thought you were the champion of small business? I thought you cared about the independent collision repairers; why would you want us to be part of a large franchise organization?"

Look, franchises may or may not be a good fit for you, but it is a great way for many shops to gain the benefits usually reserved for large MSOs and still retain one hundred percent ownership. It is still a way to achieve the American Dream, just with a little help!

Consider this for a moment: when you think of McDonald's, what comes to mind? A large corporation that is forcing small business owners out of existence? The truth is that eighty percent of the thirty-six thousand McDonald's locations worldwide are owned and operated by independent local business men and women. As mentioned in the third chapter on building a sustainable business model, many franchise organizations do a lot of the work for the franchisee when it comes to providing a proven and reliable business strategy and set of processes to ensure consistency and predictability. The franchise is a viable option to accomplish it!

Camille Eber is a successful and well-known body shop owner. She currently co-owns two locations in Oregon—Fix Auto Portland East and Fix Auto Gladstone. Camille shared her experience becoming part of the Fix Auto Network, while still operating as an independent owner.

From left to right: Iala Bray, William Bray, Camille Eber and James Bray, Fix Auto Portland East and Fix Auto Gladstone

CASE STUDY: CAMILLE EBER – FIX AUTO PORTLAND EAST AND FIX AUTO GLADSTONE

Roth & Miller Autobody was opened in 1946 by Chet Roth & C.E. Miller. My folks, Jim and Doris Eber, purchased it in 1963. I began working at the shop in 1986 and three years later decided to buy it after my mother passed away. My nephew, William Bray, became a minority partner in 2012.

We became associated with the Fix Auto Network of body shops in late 2008 after a chance crossing of paths with another of the Fix Auto Network shop owners, and franchised as a charter franchisee in 2011. Being part of the Fix Auto Network has provided us with business connections we struggled maintaining as a single shop owner and creates networking opportunities with performance-based forward-thinking shop owners I have found to be some of the best-of-the-best operators in the U.S. and beyond. It also allows for broad and rich joint marketing and advertising campaigns.

For me, aligning with Fix Auto has provided opportunities that I would not have had without their brand and the other owners in the network. This industry has phenomenal human beings who make for phenomenal operators and operations. I feel honored to be in the room with so many extraordinary men and women. If I'm struggling with something, there is always someone a phone call away who will take the time to listen and give me an opinion or advice—this can be priceless.

We have experienced unprecedented growth (for us) under the Fix Auto banner and I attribute this, in part, to our corporate staff and insurance relations department. The single-point-of-contact Fix Auto insurance relations department provides the insurer benefits the franchisees by delivering a consistent message. The performance-based tracking we share between the franchisees keeps us readily informed while allowing an arena for a level of friendly competition among the owners, as well as the locations sharing the same ownership. This is only a portion of the power I find in participating in a high-level peer group.

I don't believe I would have stepped out to acquire a second location without the corporate support, or without the drive of the next generation that is my nephew, William Bray, and our bookkeeper—his wife, Iala Bray.

This is the power of belonging to a peer group!

PERFORMANCE GROUPS

Performance groups, peer management groups, or 20 Groups, as they are sometimes referred to, are a great way to get out of your shop and away from your current bubble of beliefs! These peer groups are generally sponsored and hosted by paint manufacturers and consist of anywhere from ten to twenty non-competing collision repair shop leaders in a group.

Most groups tackle a lot of the same challenges, but you will notice some groups have a theme that eventually emerges through either the interests of its members or the facilitator. For example, my friends Mike Anderson, Larry Baker and Ron Kuehn all facilitate Axalta Performance Groups and are extremely good at what they do. Mike's groups have been reported to be very focused on the financial aspects of the business, and members probably understand how to read a financial statement better than most. Larry's groups gravitate toward leadership skills, while Ron's groups seem to focus on process improvements and cycle time. All groups do a great job covering every aspect of collision repair, but I have found some tend to highlight certain business aspects more than others. This is a good thing because it helps keep things interesting. You will also find that there are groups that specialize in different business segments such as MSOs and dealerships.

One of the industry's best-known peer group management companies, Square One Systems, runs what is known as the Coyote Vision Group. Square One Systems represents $1.2 BILLION in collision repair dollars from the shops they serve. They offer facilitation services for several different paint companies in addition to performing services for private groups.

Elainna Sachire, the company's owner, says this style of mastermind group is more important now than ever before. She believes that independent collision repairers have tremendous opportunities right now, but many shop owners are too reluctant to let go of the past. She says that the performance groups that are seeing the biggest positive changes in their businesses are those in the groups that challenge each other to think differently and to confront their old beliefs.

The beautiful thing about a well-facilitated performance group is the amount of knowledge shared among its members. Great friendships are formed and your group partners help keep you accountable for improvement efforts. The participants in most groups I know of must be voted into it by the members; therefore, you can expect some high-quality people being represented.

I recently spoke to Mike Anderson of Collision Advice about the power of peer groups, and he had this to say:

> Many times people will ask me what I think shops need to do in order to "thrive and not just survive" in the collision repair industry. I think the key to success is surrounding yourself with people who have the same positive outlook as you do. However, they will also hold you accountable and tell you when they think that what you are doing is not a good idea or a good path to pursue. Networking with your peers (like-minded individuals as well as people whose opinions may differ from yours) is critical to success in our industry. The ability to bounce ideas off of others who may have traveled this road before you or are currently on the same journey will keep you mentally prepared for what you may

encounter. The opportunity to interact with peers, both liked-minded and those with differing opinions, is most often found in 20 Group-style meetings whereas shops that are not competitors meet on a regular basis to exchange ideas in regards to the three areas that businesses need to succeed: Sales and Marketing, Production, and HR and Accounting. If I were to examine all of the shops in North America that are highly successful, their membership in this 20 Group-style of meetings would be the common thread.

While I believe that the power of peer groups is vital to the success of independent collision repairers, as I mentioned in Chapter 1, be careful of joining groups made up of small-minded or negative people. As Mike Anderson said, you want to surround yourself with people who share a "positive outlook."

When it comes to the power of peer groups, Dan Stander of Fix Auto Highlands Ranch in Littleton, Colorado is certainly a great resource on the subject. The president of ASA Colorado's collision division said that joining an association and/or advisory council offers many benefits for shop owners.

Dan grew up in the auto body business. As a young boy, he recalls sweeping floors in his grandfather's body shop in Englewood, Colorado. After working with another shop owner for a brief time, his father and mother, Jerry and Bernie, opened their own shop in February 1983—Jerry Stander's Auto Body.

The body shop became part of Fix Auto USA in 2011 and is now called Fix Auto Highlands Ranch. Dan is currently the operations manager at the family-run business, which draws on the support of over one hundred collision repair locations and includes fifteen employees.

Dan Stander

I joined ASA Colorado in 2004 and the ASA collision operations committee a year later. When I became more involved in ASA on the national level, I began learning from the great ASA staff, industry partners, vendors and veterans such as Darrel Amberson, Mike Anderson, Dan Bailey, Scott Benavidez, Jerry Burns, April Hernandez, Ron Nagy and Roy Schnepper. They are great people and have now become friends. I have learned how to deal with many different situations after hearing about their experiences.

I have also been part of the operations committee and government affairs committee with ASA national. Again, the power of learning from others.

Currently, I am the president of ASA Colorado's collision division. ASA Colorado is very strong on the mechanical side. I'm usually one of the only collision guys who shows up at the meetings. There are a lot of collision-related mechanical issues we have to deal with at the shop. Granted, we don't do maintenance, but there are a lot of different repair matters to learn from the mechanical folks at ASA Colorado that I apply to our business.

The issues ASA Colorado is currently focusing on include promoting hands-on training and finding ways to help the industry to hopefully do a better job on the vehicles and for the consumers.

I always encourage shops to get involved with associations, advisory councils and networking opportunities. Whether it's ASA, CIC or SCRS, I think industry associations are key and help you learn what's going on. I also recommend joining an advisory council. I've worked with various advisory councils over the years such as AudaExplore, Cyncast, Fix Auto, NACE and NSF, and I found that it gives you the opportunity to learn from others in the industry. Twenty Groups offered through paint companies and other vendors also help you stay educated and up-to-date on new developments. All of these offer the best networking opportunities money cannot buy.

CHAPTER 6 TAKEAWAYS

* Well-run single store shops can be highly successful.
* All of the greatest men, women and shops associate in a mastermind or peer group.
* Join an association of success-minded shop leaders; avoid pity-parties.
* Women (and even men) should join the Women's Industry Network.
* Consider a franchise if it's a good fit for you and your shop.
* See the website www.bodyshopsecrets.com/resources for more information on peer groups.

Chapter 7

● ● ●

THE FUTURE OF COLLISION REPAIR

"Don't Wish Things Were Easier,
Wish You Were Better."

– JIM ROHN

The future of our business seems so uncertain, so daunting, yet at the same time so exciting! People ask me all the time for my opinion about the future of collision repair. Will consolidation continue? Will technology eliminate the need for repair shops? While I don't think it is possible to predict all these things with great accuracy, I do have some thoughts on these questions that may interest you.

PART ONE
FUTURE CONSOLIDATION

As long as private equity or Wall Street finds the collision repair business a safe and lucrative investment, consolidators will continue to grow—at least for a while. I do believe, however, that the number of metropolitan statistical areas in the United States that are still ripe for the picking is starting to dwindle, so consolidators will be forced to start moving outside of their comfort zone to look for different ways to continue growth. This could include acquiring more single locations instead of focusing on only buying medium- to large-sized MSOs, and it could also mean more brownfields and even greenfields in order to build new locations where insurance partners need them the most. Industry experts have been predicting one of the big guys buying out another big guy, and I agree this course of action seems to make sense, but we shall see. Or perhaps an even bigger player will emerge that we aren't currently familiar with?

All four big consolidators—ABRA, Boyd/Gerber, Caliber and Service King—have announced that they will double in size over the next few years, and some experts predict they will acquire as much as twenty percent of all claims volume in the United States by 2020. The future level of success of our country's consolidators also depends on you! I hope this book is inspiring some of you to rethink your motives to sell, and maybe instead inspire you to grow and build an even more amazing independently-owned business. If you want to sell because you want out for the right reasons, sell! If you want to sell because you are nervous about the future, and have some self-doubts, remember you are more powerful than you know.

People in the world love to talk about consolidation from a victim's perspective. We talk about Wall Street and private equity and the insurance industry support that is driving consolidation, but we often forget to talk about the most important factor—the customer. Despite insurance company steering, our consumers still have the freedom to choose a repairer that best suits their needs. What are you doing to differentiate the customers' experience at your shop compared to the experience they would have at a consolidator shop? Why should a consumer choose you? Don't make the fatal assumption that all consolidator shops aren't good at it because many of them are. However, you can be even better. Ultimately, it is the consumer that gets to dictate the growth of a company— yours or the consolidators. As independent collision repairers, we must stop blaming consolidation for our failure to provide an exceptional customer experience. Whoever get this right, wins!

FUTURE AUTOMOBILE TECHNOLOGY

What would happen to the collision repair industry if automobile collisions no longer happened? This is a serious concern to many in our industry and I hear a lot of differing opinions on the subject. Clearly, crash avoidance technology is already a reality. Many speculate that it will soon become standard equipment on most vehicles, and I don't find any reason to doubt it given the progress we are already seeing. I am positive that such technology will create the intended safety consumers seek in their automobile purchases, and it will have a dramatic effect on the number of vehicles that need to be repaired. I believe that if it were not for the increased use of cell phones and other distractions by drivers in the past few years, we would have already felt a steeper decline in repair work than we already have. As I said earlier, I don't have a crystal ball to predict the future, but I don't think we need one to know that vehicle accident frequency will likely decrease and we may end up having a surplus of shops as a result.

Now before you go and jump off a bridge, let me point out a couple of things. There is always an opportunity contained in every adversity. Despite the decrease in the number of repairs and crash severity, many believe as do I, that the cost to repair relative to severity could likely increase. This is due to the additional technology involved as well as the expense to repair it. As I write this, there are serious conversations taking place throughout the industry about the added expense of diagnostic scanning, both before and after repairs, as well as many other calibrations that are required. Yes, fixing cars will continue to require new skills, new equipment and new expenses, but for the shops with the right mindset to weather the technological storm, I think a very prosperous future could be in store. Sadly, some shops will not survive. There is no use blaming "big business" for the decline in the number of shops in this country; it is a simple and natural matter of survival of the fittest, and it happens in most industries. If you embrace the change and apply some of the lessons suggested in this book, you will not only survive but benefit and prosper from our quickly changing world.

THE FUTURE OF SELF-DRIVING CARS

What about autonomous vehicles? I believe that self-driving cars are indeed a reality of our future, mainly because they already exist. The big questions that remain unanswered are how long will it take to perfect the technology for practical use, and how long before humans embrace it from a consumer standpoint?

While the concept of the driverless car has been around for nearly a century, in 2009 Google decided to make it a priority. While Google has no interest in becoming a car manufacturer, the company has been relentless in its pursuit of the perfect autonomous car. Logging millions of miles, Google, several vehicle manufacturers, and even UBER, are working on some impressive developments with the technology and learning very quickly how to make self-driving a reality. UBER is already running autonomous cars all over the city streets of Pittsburgh, Pennsylvania, while Google's friendly-looking Google car that has no interior driving controls whatsoever has been seen all over our roads with only minor negative results. These cars utilize a combination of lasers, cameras and radar technology to identify objects and then respond accordingly. Proponents of the technology say that it will save lives by reducing cars crashes, reduce traffic congestion, and give people with disabilities access to transportation they may not have otherwise.

No one can seem to give an exact answer to our tough question though. How long until it affects the collision repair industry? I hear answers that range anywhere from three to thirty years, but I am not losing any sleep over it. I do not believe autonomous cars will completely replace cars with drivers anytime soon because other than being stuck in traffic, many of us still love to drive. The technology, while possibly providing more safety than with a distracted human driver, is currently in a stage of what Google calls "paranoia." The vehicles are learning very quickly how to identify objects and react appropriately, but there is a lot of learning still to be done before these computer-driven cars do it with confidence. It is like a nervous teenager just learning how to drive, paying very careful attention, but never willing to risk pulling out into traffic and trusting that the oncoming car will slow down. I would hate to be the guy stuck behind one of these cars attempting to pull out into busy traffic! There are other limitations too. As of now, the sensing technology has difficulty working in inclement weather and is useless on snow-covered roads.

I believe when self-driving cars do become widely available to the public, they will initially be targeting carpool type-transportation, the elderly, and those with disabilities. I am excited to watch as this technology unfolds and hopefully makes the world a better place, instead of just being another useless gadget.

LEARNING OUR FUTURE FROM OTHER COUNTRIES

Several years ago, I kept hearing stories about this English guy who was traveling around America with a coaching and consulting program called "Advocate." Everyone was telling me that Mike Monaghan had a very similar business model to my own and that I needed to meet him. Through a mutual friend, the introduction was made and Mike and I quickly became great friends. One thing that made Mike such a valuable resource to the collision industry in our country was his uncanny ability to predict trends and to understand the path that had led to collision repairers' current challenges. Although he is one of the smartest guys I know, it wasn't his intelligence as much as it was his keen observations of the same challenges that had already taken place in his country that gave him this amazing insight.

Mike's insight was extremely valuable and helped me understand what has caused many of the problems we are currently experiencing in our country and what can and can't be done about it. Almost any challenge you can think of that we are experiencing in America has already happened in the United Kingdom—ten or more years ago. Suppressed labor rates? Check! Consolidation? Been there, done that! The good news is that some of the solutions we need can also be found by paying attention to what the survivors have already done in the United Kingdom.

Mike is quick to point out that while watching for trends in other countries is smart, you must be careful. The United States is a very different country from the U.K. in several respects. The way things unfolded over there is not the same way it will likely unfold here. Still, bright minds will occasionally look outside of both their bubble and their country to gain insight on what could happen in the future here in America. It won't take place the same way, but certain events will definitively occur in a similar fashion.

If you think we have problems here in the U.S., you will wonder how our friends over the pond have even survived with what they've had to deal with. Their prevailing labor rates are ridiculously low. There are accident management companies that act as middlemen between shops and insurers. These companies are allowed to keep large percentages of the already thin margins for their services. Did I mention that most shops must provide free courtesy cars? Shop space, parking and things that many of us take for granted here in the U.S. are hard to come by for most shops in the U.K. With the challenges they have faced, it's no wonder so many have not survived, and most that have survived are lucky to generate a profit of more than a percentage point or two.

Happily, there are some exceptions. A handful of shops in the U.K. have applied many of the same principles found in this book, and through refocusing on the customer experience instead of being completely dependent on insurance contracts, they are thriving. Many of these same outliers are also discovering amazing new ways of processing high-quality repairs and achieving continuous workflow through better thinking and technology. These are the positive deviants that we can learn a lot from if we pay careful attention to what they are doing. During a recent conversation with Mike, he reported a current shift of power leaning back towards the U.K. shops: consolidation is slowing and independent shops are once again beginning to prosper.

I know things are challenging in the collision repair industry and I really am sympathetic, but not for the reasons you might think. We live in a free country that is so abundant with opportunities, and yet far too many people have long forgotten how blessed we are. We take so much for granted. I am not sympathetic because things are difficult. I am sympathetic because so many people live in the fog of the victim zone and they don't know any better. Anything that is worthwhile in this life is never easy, and greatness was never achieved by things being easy! Perhaps a visit to a foreign country may be the cure for some?

In many global markets, shops have surpassed a majority of Americans in terms of technology and process methodology due to what I like to call "forced discipline." These guys are not necessarily smarter than Americans; it is just that many of them have been forced to improve as a matter of survival. People tend to get very innovative when their lives depend on it! Topics that are now mainstream in our country have been a reality in other parts of the world for quite some time. The recent news we hear at industry events such as diagnostic scanning, using OEM repair methods, and shop OEM certification is old news in other countries, including the U.K.

THE FUTURE OF COLLISION REPAIR SYSTEMS

What fascinates me greatly in the U.K. are the advancements made in developing systems to make continuous workflow possible. When you have limited parking and running out of loaner cars, the reduction of work in process and improved cycle time becomes a priority. Shops in other countries have developed very smart systems that will allow vehicle repairs to flow continuously through the shop without all of the usual delays we have grown accustomed to. Some of the production systems that you have heard about in this book that are being used by America's greatest body shops were first developed overseas.

During a meeting in Nashville, Tennessee with Mike Monaghan in 2014, I was introduced to another British gentleman by the name of Jon Parker. This chance introduction has since evolved into a very meaningful friendship and the personal adoption of a new and improved philosophy on production methodologies.

Since first learning of Theory of Constraints in the 1990s from reading Eliyahu Goldratt's and Jeff Cox's book, *The Goal,* I have made what some may consider significant advancements with collision repair production systems. In recent years, I combined my knowledge of Theory of Constraints methods with many years as a Lean practitioner and spent countless hours on the shop floor perfecting my version of the perfect system. I felt as though I understood our industry's closest possible version of continuous workflow—that is until the afternoon I met Jon Parker.

I had heard of Jon and followed his work through articles I had read in recent years, so I was quite excited to have the opportunity to meet him and compare notes. Jon was a reputed Theory of Constraints expert and the founder of Bodyshop Revolution, a U.K. company bringing exciting new processes and technology to North America. This chance afternoon encounter quickly turned into a very late evening as I once again became the eager student, soaking up as much information as I could.

Jon shared a quote with me that I will never forget: "The trouble with collision repairers is that they spend a lot of time trying to do the wrong things, righter." He then used the analogy of improving a bicycle. "You can spend years improving your bicycle and getting better at riding a bicycle and eventually even become the fastest bicycle rider in the city, but you will never be as fast as a Formula One race car." He then went on to ask, "How nice would it be if you could just forget everything you know about how automobiles are supposed to be processed, and just start with a clean slate? Because that is exactly what I've done!"

"The trouble with collision repairers is that they spend a lot of time trying to do the wrong things, righter." – Jon Parker

Jon explained to me how he and his team threw out all the rules and started over to create a system free of old, stale thinking that would make the Holy Grail of continuous workflow a reality. Instead of adding more departments like we have been doing in many of our country's lean shops, he was removing departments. Rather than creating efficient silos using commissioned technicians, Jon focused only on global efficiency. Eventually, on paper they had created the best possible system, but then Jon still needed to prove it.

Because the concept was so radically different from traditional body shop models in the U.K. or anywhere else for that matter, to prove out the concept Jon and his team would need to build their own shop from the ground up. Attempting to convert an existing business to this type of thinking would take too long. The new shop quickly proved out the concept and with the help of catalytic drying robotics, was turning over forty cars a week in a production space of just over six thousand square feet.

Since proving out the concept in the U.K., Jon Parker and Bodyshop Revolution have been making an impact with their process and technology in English-speaking countries around the world. Several of America's greatest body shops, including LaMettry's in Minnesota and Rydell Collision Center in North Dakota, have reported great quality and throughput improvements using this system.

With American business partner, Patrick O'Neil, Bodyshop Revolution introduced Bodyshop Express in San Diego, California. Using Catalytic Drying robots from Greentech Dryers, roll-on primers, and the other Bodyshop Revolution process methodologies, the Express Shop is now producing over fifty cars a week through a single paint booth, no prep deck, and with cycle times less than four days on average.

I will admit that Bodyshop Revolution is not for everybody, but I think for disciplined shop owners who are looking for a better way to produce high-quality repairs, faster than ever before, and with fewer hassles, there is no other system I know of in the United States that compares. But, I will also tell you that some shops may purchase robotic drying systems with the expectation that they will fix all of your problems. They won't! They will dry paint faster than anything you have ever seen, but they won't fix bad leadership or poor processes. For shops to take full advantage of this technology, they have to get the basics right first. For example, if a shop is not analyzing damage correctly, a robot will not help. The Holy Grail of collision repair is to produce high-quality repair work with continuous flow. Bodyshop Revolution will provide that, but only if the shop is disciplined enough to avoid falling into the trap of old thinking and instead diligently stick to the proven process.

*From left to right: Patrick O'Neil, owner of
Bodyshop Express, with Dave Luehr*

PART TWO

In addition to the catalytic drying robotic technology, there are other new forms of technology I have been keeping an eye on that show a lot of promise and I believe will become commonplace in the successful body shops of the future. If you visit our website's resource page, www.bodyshopsecrets.com/resources, you will find more information about how to contact the suppliers of this technology.

AS-TECH

The asTech™ device is a remote diagnostic tool that allows collision shops and repair technicians to have a vehicle scanned before or after repair work is done. Scanning ensures that all the vehicle's issues have been fully addressed and that all systems are working properly. The cool thing about this device is that it connects the vehicle in your shop via the Internet to a technician at Collision Diagnostic Services, using a factory scan tool. After you purchase the asTech device, there is a per use fee. It is currently being used by many of my clients and has captured dozens of diagnostic trouble codes that may have gone unnoticed without it. My clients report they have been able to reduce unwanted trips to the dealership dramatically.

LEANTEC

LeanTec Inventory Solutions has revolutionized how shops can manage their paint and body supply inventory. I have been collaborating with Lean Tec's founder, Brandon Clift, for several years as he has been developing this technology and I am very impressed with the finished product line. This innovative system has been designed to help secure, track and invoice materials. LeanTec makes it easy to maintain accountability and to accurately control processes, which will lead to dramatic cost reductions. The technology utilizes both stationary cabinets and mobile carts to store inventory securely and accurately keep track of usage. This cloud-based solution offers automated replenishment in real-time.

BODYSHOP BOOSTER

Bodyshop Booster is a mobile app that allows current and future customers to send high-quality damage images to body shops with guided instructions. This technology has great marketing capabilities for shops seeking to stand out from the competition. I have worked with the company's founder, Ryan Taylor, to learn how shops can use this technology operationally and discovered that in addition to its value as a marketing and communication tool, it has vast potential to improve operational performance. High-performance shops seeking a better way to triage or schedule damaged vehicles smarter will benefit greatly from incorporating Bodyshop Booster into their systems.

THE FUTURE OF DAMAGE ANALYSIS

The traditional method of performing quick, curb-written estimates has to stop. Automobiles are too advanced, and getting more so. Poorly-written estimates continue to be the breeding ground of many bad habits, process failures and even sub-standard quality. Other than capturing the occasional "shopper" who is searching for private pay work, I can think of only a few benefits to writing drive-in "guesstimates."

Most shops in our country continue to write guesstimates and then pre-order the parts based on the inaccurate appraisal, and even order some additional "just-in-case" parts. Then they schedule the customer in for a repair appointment where the vehicle is torn down, and additional damage is discovered, and a supplement is created—usually multiple supplements. On the day that the vehicle is scheduled to be delivered back to the customer, they decide to finally hook up a scan tool to find out why that pesky dash warning light is still on, only to discover that the vehicle has serious mechanical or electrical issues that will either cause delays, additional expense, or possibly even total loss the vehicle. Such is the day in the life of a typical body shop. Traditional methods can cause devastation to the entire repair process including delays, additional man-hours and general chaos. It's time for something different!

At the slightly more advanced body shops, let's call them "next-level shops," many have implemented what they consider a blueprinting program designed to capture a more accurate repair plan prior to releasing the vehicle into production. Unfortunately, many of these shop's blueprinting efforts are little more than an attempt to write a better supplement. These next-level shops have merely scratched the surface of how proper damage analysis should be performed and many quickly abandon their blueprinting efforts and revert to allowing technicians to write the supplements for them, one part at a time.

America's greatest body shops are taking a different approach—an approach that I believe is the correct path for shops to prosper in the future. These shops understand that to diagnose a damaged modern automobile properly, it takes a little time, a good, repeatable process, and discipline. As with many aspects of lean thinking, you must invest time up front if you want to reap the rewards of quality, speed and profits later on.

The greatest shops are now rethinking how they staff their businesses. Many are favoring the elimination of technically-skilled estimators in customer-facing positions, and utilizing people in the front office who are experts in customer service. Some shops are moving away from unscheduled drive-in estimates altogether. Highly-trained damage analysts take positions on the shop floor in dedicated blueprinting areas where activities include disassembly and proper diagnosis, which requires pre-scanning every vehicle for diagnostic trouble codes. Each vehicle has a repair plan specifically created that incorporates the vehicle manufacturer's recommended repair methods. If calibrations are needed to correct vehicle functions, these professionals will discover them during the blueprinting process and write them into the repair plan, instead of discovering them on Friday afternoon when the customer is on the way to pick up the vehicle.

Another variation to analyzing damage that I have found very effective is a system already being used successfully at several of America's greatest body shops and widely used in the U.K. It is called Vehicle Damage Appraisal, or V.D.A. I believe as technology and reduced cycle time expectations continue to increase, you will see similar appraisal systems begin to emerge on a larger scale in America.

The method is used on drivable cars where the customer is scheduled for an appraisal appointment that lasts approximately forty-five minutes. The process begins by understanding the proper repair methods and utilizing OEM information to do so. Cars are scanned for diagnostic trouble codes and minor disassembly is performed (usually while the customer is in the waiting room), then safely reassembled. Assuming there are no safety concerns, the customer is put back in the drivable car until all of the correct parts have arrived and a date is scheduled to start the repairs immediately.

Some people, upon first hearing of this system, are quick to discount its effectiveness, citing the many reasons it won't work, instead of trying it first. For certain individuals, it might be hard to imagine spending the time and utilizing the resources to implement a V.D.A. or similar appraisal method, because it is truly a significant commitment. But time and time again, the shops that are willing to challenge their beliefs are finding great success with this system and positive things usually come from efforts made outside of someone's comfort zone.

Blueprinting is still the popular choice and understandably so for many successful shops. However, no system I have seen will reduce unwanted vehicle inventory and allow smaller jobs to continuously flow through the shop, as compared to what I have seen with this new approach to drivable vehicle appraisal.

THE FUTURE WORKFORCE

As discussed in Chapter 5, the technician shortage continues to be a leading topic at industry events. It's not only the collision industry that is suffering right now; it's commonplace in most trades that require physical labor. We are fighting a social conditioning dilemma and I am sickened by what our children are being brought up to believe—the belief that entering a trade where those who use their hands to earn a living is somehow unworthy. This is a ludicrous point of view from small-minded people who think everyone in the world needs to attend a four-year college and then enter a career that involves wearing a white collar. Who's going to do the work? Who's going to build cool stuff?

Society is going to do what society does, and I don't think my opinion or this book is going to change that very much. I do want to make a small difference, and I want to ask all of you to do your part to inspire young people to come into the collision repair industry. Together we can make positive changes, but first, as an industry, we must take accountability for our failure to provide a workplace that people want to come to work. Many people, and especially our youth, are hungry to make a difference in the world, and we must ask ourselves, "Does the collision industry provide that opportunity?" I don't believe as an industry we always communicate effectively to our young people, or maybe the message is somehow getting lost. The bottom line is that a lot of work needs to be done.

What most of us truly want from life is to be happy, right? What kind of work helps people be happy? Meaningful work. Nowhere is it written that the skilled trades is not meaningful work! Building stuff for people, fixing things for people, and using your hands to create is as meaningful as anything I can think of doing. I asked Brandon Eckenrode, the director of development at Collision Repair Education Foundation, what he would advise others in the industry to do to support this message.

Through working at the Collision Repair Education Foundation (CREF), I have had the opportunity to visit high school and college collision school programs across the country and have seen both successful programs and others that are in need of help. Those that are successful have a very active and engaged local industry supporting these programs by serving on their collision advisory board, organizing local fundraisers for their program, are actively engaged with their students/instructors, and are visible with the school administration. When the schools can regularly see the many different types of businesses that are interested in their collision students, I believe it helps showcase a need of not only keeping the collision programs open, but also supporting them with a reasonable program budget. Local industry businesses visiting with the students, hosting field trips to their businesses, and showcasing to administrators/counselors that there are future career paths for the students, will help on many different levels.

The local industry engagement needs to also start at a younger age. Even showcasing the industry at the grade school level can't hurt as it introduces the industry to the students and potentially the parents who are going to have an active role guiding their students' future choices. When most people think of the collision industry, they don't understand that there are a countless number of career opportunities outside of an insurance adjuster and collision repair technician. Career opportunities include administration, customer relations, IT, marketing, public relations, sales, and much more. If the collision industry doesn't take the lead and gather on a nationwide scale to showcase itself as a provider of a successful future for students, we run the risk of losing great candidates to other technical trades and industries. I regularly attend the American School Counselor Association annual conference and have an opportunity to present to kindergarten/high school counselors. This industry needs to be aware of the fact that the other technical trades are in the same situation our industry is in (aged workforce) and they are eager to attract students to their industry just as much as we are. Now, more than ever, is the time for the collision industry to organize and come together in becoming a more visible career option for students.

TRAINING FOR THE FUTURE

Education in the old days was the gap between performers and non-performers. That is no longer the case. Anything you want to know is available with the touch of a button! Not knowing how to do something is no longer a good excuse. Industry organizations, such as the Automotive Management Institute (AMi), offer online classes on almost any subject relating to the operation and management of an automotive repair business. Our industry has also seen great improvements with accessibility to technical training solutions through I-CAR, the Inter-Industry Conference on Auto Collision Repair. Both organizations have informative websites, and online training can be accessed in mere moments for shops wanting to improve their skills. See our resource page: www.bodyshopsecrets.com/resources.

TECHNICAL TRAINING

Technical training has become more important than ever, and shops that do not invest in training technicians to properly repair today's vehicles are putting customers and their businesses at risk. A big problem in our industry that I have discovered through my volunteer activities with I-CAR is that many body shops still consider the training as something that needs to be done to remain compliant with their insurance direct repair program requirements and only put in just enough effort to remain compliant. This is a dangerous attitude! America's greatest body shops view technical training as an integral part of operational success. They do it because it's the right thing to do, not because it's required by their insurance partners.

In my role as a coach and consultant to body shops, I walk through many, many shops and am seeing a repetitive problem—expensive equipment collecting dust. Many shops buy the equipment to qualify for various OEM certifications or DRP programs, but many of these programs don't enforce the requirement that the technicians actually use it. When I interview technicians to discover why it isn't being used, the usual answer is that they don't know how, or they haven't used the equipment often enough to operate it confidently. The technicians commonly accuse the equipment manufacturers for the lack of training, but I believe the problem is a combination of the manufacturers' minimal training at delivery plus a general lack of interest at the shops by both leadership and technicians.

The equipment I am speaking of is aluminum repair equipment, dent pulling equipment, plastic nitrogen welders, spot welders, bronze-silicone welding equipment, and more. This equipment is designed to help shops properly repair today's high-tech vehicles and far too many shops aren't using it! It is time to embrace this technology and train technicians how to not only turn on the machines, but to use them proficiently and confidently.

To me, proper technical training, and becoming an I-CAR Gold Class shop is table stakes. You need it just to play the game! Once you are in the game, however, a different type of training is needed to differentiate yourself from the competition. The skills I am referring to are the kind you will find through organizations such as AMi. Throughout this book, you have been learning some of these skills: leadership, financial, the customer experience, and so on. The successful shops of the future will need to proactively pursue training in all of these areas if they want to prosper.

One area in particular that most shops are poor at and would benefit from training is simply the interaction with the customer. Most believe they are "good enough," but my experience indicates a great deal of improvement is needed. As one of the most critical parts of our business, far too many shops place a low-paid, untrained (and sometimes unhappy) person at the front lines with the potential customer. This is insanity!

During a recent discussion, Jeff Peevy, the president of the Automotive Management Institute, had this to say about it:

One of the things that I believe is missing and something honestly I have missed for most of my career and I believe the industry misses is the education of its customer-facing staff.

The lack of connection between management training and NPS (net promoter score) to me, speaks to an area we are addressing at AMi. I believe there is a void of training specific to customer-facing employees. It is important

THE SECRETS OF AMERICA'S GREATEST BODY SHOPS

that technicians be trained to do their part of a complete, safe and quality repair, while customer-facing employees be aware of and practice customer-service skills, including face-to-face and telephone skills, and multiple-facing communications skills. In fact, I would challenge the industry to consider the often "forgotten front office staff" and take a serious look at it. Some have said to me that employee turnover with office staff is too great to invest in their training, but I would say part of the reason they leave is they see they are not invested in like technicians and estimators. I believe it is the next training frontier as shops work to take their customer satisfaction and performance to the next level. We have positioned the next generation of AMi, a neutral educational nonprofit, to lead and collaborate with the industry in that aspect of training.

For more information about I-CAR and AMi, see our resource page: www.bodyshopsecrets.com/resources.

CONCLUSION

Shortly after founding Elite Body Shop Solutions in 2013, it became apparent that my dream of helping the independent collision repairer by offering the world's greatest Lean and Theory of Constraints repair processes was not enough. As many coaches and consultants before me have discovered, a business owner who does not have the right mindset or leadership skills cannot be helped very much by being offered process solutions, management tools or magic pills intended to fix their operational problems. I discovered that if I were going to be true to my mission of helping shops survive and prosper, I would need an approach that would first involve opening the mind of the business owner and offering leadership and personal development education before my process solutions would be effective for the long term.

Little did I know only a few short years ago that uncovering the real needs of the collision repair community would lead me on a journey of learning the cognitive functions of the human mind. I often found myself in the unfamiliar and sometimes uncomfortable space of learning something new that seemed to have absolutely nothing to do with the successful operation of a body shop, yet had everything to do with it. I was reminded of my deviation from the traditional on occasion by fellow industry leaders. One friend even told me that I needed to give up all the psycho-babble and get back to the body shop world! While comments like this stung a little, I was also familiar with the levels of stress and dysfunction in the shops being run by the individuals making the comments. It only made me more determined to crack the code to figure out what makes body shop people highly successful.

Human potential is so vast, beautiful and amazing that I am constantly inspired to help those in the collision repair industry discover and embrace theirs. This is not always an easy task, as many are burdened with negative thinking and belief systems that are difficult to breach.

Unleashing this potential begins with individuals having the courage to look in the mirror and admit that they alone are responsible for everything both good and bad that is happening in their lives. Being fully accountable for one's life is both frightening and extremely freeing.

What has been so refreshing about working with some of the impressive people who have been included in the pages of this book is their level of self-accountability and their shared passion for learning new things. Many of them, as I do, view the discovery of problems as opportunities to increase both performance and knowledge. Feedback and criticism are embraced, not avoided, and failure, if not celebrated, is at least viewed opportunistically. This attitude, I believe, is at the very foundation of the success of America's greatest body shops, and because of this attitude, all the other success principles mentioned in this book become possible.

For those who have read this book, I congratulate you for your commitment to learning. Chances are very good that you have the right stuff to reach your personal potential. If for some reason after reading this book you have discovered that you have a lot of work to do and perhaps even feel overwhelmed, I understand and can relate. The journey of personal and business development is never-ending and it is best to get comfortable being uncomfortable. Having said that, there are simple actions that you can take to continually move towards your lofty goals without feeling overwhelmed—primarily goal setting and time-management skills.

Learning to set goals and managing time is not something we were typically taught in school, or by our parents, so it is a skill that most people have to acquire on their own. It is usually one of the very first things I teach my body shop clients because it is the foundational knowledge that makes everything else possible. That is why I will share a few of these skills as a way to conclude this book and get you started on the next leg of your journey in the best way possible.

Most people either fail to set goals, or if they do set them, they quickly fail to follow through. There are several reasons for this, but here is one primary reason—*they don't know how* to achieve really big, meaningful goals. It's not always a *will* problem, as much as it is a *skill* problem.

Let me explain how this works. When people sit down to write their goals, they typically use what is called the S.M.A.R.T. formula, meaning they will set goals that are Specific, Measurable, Attainable, Realistic, Timely. In other words... B.O.R.I.N.G! This system works great for things like project management, but rarely works well for creating meaningful and compelling dreams that will both inspire and create the necessary passion to follow through. One of the reasons people typically set small, "realistic" goals is because they are using their <u>current</u> knowledge bank to determine the feasibility of the goal they are setting. They are setting future goal achievement based only on what they have already learned, instead of what they <u>could</u> learn in the future. This behavior is extremely limiting and one of the main reasons so many fail or have given up on goal setting in the first place.

In the past, knowledge may have been attainable, but it could be difficult to get. Sometimes, it required formal education or several trips to the local library. In today's connected world, almost any piece of information can be obtained with the simple push of a button! You can learn more now in one week over the Internet than what would have taken months or even years to learn a few, short years ago.

When you accept the realization that everything you could possibly want to know is already available somewhere, <u>and</u> you apply courage in your goal setting, you will discover that almost anything is possible!

PRACTICAL APPLICATION

Now that I have shared this high-level concept for attaining one's dreams and goals, let's take it down to the shop floor level and apply it. The secret here is that instead of analyzing your current knowledge bank before you set goals, you set goals first and then figure out what you will need to learn in order to get there. Simple, right? Here is my four-step approach.

FOUR-STEP APPROACH TO GOAL SETTING

1. Big goal – What is my big scary goal?
2. Intermediate goal(s) – What things need to happen to reach that big scary goal?
3. Daily tasks – What steps can I accomplish today to support my intermediate goal(s)?
4. What do I need to learn to support my goals? (These also become part of your daily task routine.)

Here is an example: (Keep in mind this is a very basic example, and in reality, doubling your shop's revenue would likely involve many more intermediate goals, but hopefully you get the point).

1. Big scary goal:
   * Double my shop's revenue this year over the previous year
2. Intermediate goals: (This is "what needs to happen")
   * Find additional staffing
     o Begin recruiting campaign
   * Create shop capacity and efficiencies capable of doubling throughput
     o Dry paint faster to utilize booth space better
     o Create written operational playbook
   * Develop marketing strategy to bring in more work
     o Word-of-mouth marketing system
     o Develop better company branding identity
3. Daily tasks (This is "how we make it happen") a few examples...
   * Talk to current employees about helping find more technicians

* Call Elite Body Shop Solutions to develop operational playbook
* Set up meeting with branding and marketing company

4. What do I need to learn? (These also are added to your calendar as a daily task or perhaps even an intermediate goal)
   * What systems will dry paint faster? – research catalytic paint drying
   * I know nothing about how to "brand my company," where do I learn more?
   * How can I streamline my operations? – Buy a book about lean manufacturing, hire a consultant, take an online class.

Every week, you should review your intermediate goals and plug the daily tasks into your calendar or to-do list. If you make the time to take small steps each day, you will be amazed how quickly you can achieve great things!

There are many resources available today simply by going online and using a search engine like Google. When you want a dependable and trusted training resource, I like to start with AMi (Automotive Management Institute) for training on anything administrative, managerial or operational in your shop. For technical training, I-CAR remains your best source. Books are an amazing resource too because almost anything you want to know, you can find in a book! I try to read two to three books a month and have for many years, and I credit much of what I know to the books I read. It wouldn't hurt to add "read more books" to your list of goals. We will include a listing of book recommendations on our book's resource pages at www. bodyshopsecrets.com/resources.

In closing, Stacey and I want to thank you for reading *The Secrets of America's Greatest Body Shops.* If you have found value in this book, please tell a friend or colleague.

> *"Do not limit the majesty of your dreams to your current level of competence. Know that all the education you need will be available along your journey."*
> *– Dave Luehr*

ABOUT THE AUTHORS

DAVE LUEHR

With over thirty years of expertise developing the profitability and efficiency of collision repair shops, Dave Luehr combines
his decades as a body shop owner with
experience gained at some of America's
leading collision repair organizations as
founder of Elite Body Shop Solutions.
Based in Nashville, Tennessee, the business

development and professional coaching organization redefines
the value and competitive advantage collision repair businesses
can expect from an industry advisor.

As an expert writer and keynote speaker, Dave has inspired
international audiences and helped thousands improve both
their businesses and quality of life. He has also served on several
industry association boards across the country and specializes in
Lean and Theory of Constraints methods.

Contact Dave at: dluehr@bodyshopsecrets.com.

STACEY PHILLIPS

Stacey is the owner of Radiant Writing & Communications in San Diego, California. She has more than twenty years of experience editing and writing for a wide range of businesses and fields. These include technical industries such as automotive, engineering and oil and gas, as well as consumer-focused magazines, newspapers and websites. As the prior assistant editor at *Autobody News* magazine, she currently writes monthly columns and articles for the publication related to collision repair.

The award-winning writer is a graduate of the University of Southern California with a double major in Journalism and Political Science. She graduated magna cum laude and earned an Honors Thesis in Environmental Politics. In 2000, she co-authored a history book for the Institute of Chartered Accountants of Alberta.

Contact Stacey at: sphillips@bodyshopsecrets.com.

Made in the USA
Las Vegas, NV
13 September 2021